Legal Almanac Series No. 9

SEXUAL CONDUCT AND THE LAW

by **GERHARD O. W. MUELLER**
with the assistance of
Neville Ross

*This Legal Almanac has been revised
by the Oceana Editorial Staff*

Irving J. Sloan
General Editor

SECOND EDITION

1980 Oceana Publications, Inc.
Dobbs Ferry, New York 10522

Library of Congress Cataloging in Publication Data

Mueller, Gerhard O.W.
 Sexual conduct and the law.

 (Legal almanac series; no. 9)
 "This legal almanac has been revised by the Oceana
editorial staff, Irving J. Sloan, general editor."
 First ed. published in 1961 under title: Legal
regulation of sexual conduct.
 Includes index.
 1. Sex crimes--United States--States. I. Title.
KF9325.Z9M8 1979   345.73'0253   79-28180
ISBN 0-379-11129-2

Manufactured in the United States of America.

TABLE OF CONTENTS

TABLES

FOREWORD

"Law"

My remarks must first be directed to the various words which I have incorporated in the title. I speak of *legal* regulations, and this necessarily refers to the *law*. Sexual conduct, like most human activities in the United States, is subject to positive law on three levels. First, it is the governments of the various states, (including the Commonwealth of Puerto Rico and the District of Columbia) which may subject our conduct to restraint. This book addresses itself principally to such state laws, applicable only within the boundaries of each state, with exceptions not here relevant.

But activities also may be governed by the criminal law of the federal government, and in the sexual sphere the White Slave Traffic Act (so-called Mann Act) which prohibits the transportation of female persons across state lines for the purpose of prostitution, debauchery or any other immoral purpose, is a prime example.

Lastly, municipal governments have the power, by ordinance, to regulate the conduct of people within their territory. In the sexual sphere such activities as prostitution, soliciting, indecent exposure, or lewd and indecent conduct, are likely to be punishable under city ordinances. This book will not attempt to deal with municipal law.

While the tradition of our law has been the judge-made (or common) law, which is not to be found in codes of law, these traditions have been abandoned in criminal law, and as to sexual offenses, almost without exception, the law is to be found in statutes and codes. It is these to which the tables refer.

No code of law is self-explanatory, and particularly none written by lawyers steeped in the traditions of the common law. The codifier employs — without explanation — many technical terms which have derived their meaning through centuries of judicial interpretation. A single word in a statute, thus, may incorporate by reference a whole body of customary law. Many terms which convey seemingly clear meanings to laymen have acquired technical definitions with which the layman is not conversant. And, in addition, there is the law's professional jargon which is entirely meaningless to the layman. Obviously, I cannot promise within the confines of this volume to elucidate all these multifarious hidden meanings, but to the extent necessary for the understanding of the crimes here discussed, I shall attempt to do so.

Laws change constantly, whether by legislative fiat or by significant decisions of high courts. This volume, thus, is bound to be outdated as soon as it is published. But if this consideration were in the minds of all writers on law, nobody would ever publish a law book!

Lastly, law in its most specific sense—as here used—refers to the official description of that human conduct which is singled out for special official attention. The special official attention of the criminal law, of course, is punishment. A crime, or a criminal offense, then, is such conduct as is prohibited by law under threat of punishment to be inflicted by the state.

Sexual Offenses

There is by no means unanimity of agreement among the experts on what is encompassed by the term *sexual offenses*. Many sexual offenses, to be quite sure, are so obviously sexual in scope as to leave no reason for doubt. But even here caution must be exercised. Prostitution, as a sexual offense, quite frequently may be practiced for reasons which have nothing to do with the sexual gratification of

2

the prostitute and, as a matter of fact, the harm of prostitution reaches far beyond the mere injury to the moral standards of society. One need think only of the threat to public health, and the financial support for organized crime, inherent in prostitution. Thus, I suppose, the element of sexual gratification—in the psycho-physiological sense—does not necessarily enter the definition of the sexual offense. This is even clearer in pornography, where the purveyor surely acts solely for reasons of financial gain.

But some offenders derive sexual gratification from offenses which on the surface have no relation to sexual conduct. Kleptomaniacs and pyromaniacs may serve as examples. According to prevailing phychiatric theory, the kleptomaniac is a compulsive thief who steals in order to replace unrelated sexual guilt feelings by more obvious reasons for experiencing guilt. Beyond that, cases have been known where the act of theft, or of fleeing from the scene, or of being apprehended, was accompanied by sexual excitement. In even more obvious cases the thief may employ the stolen object as a *fetish* for sexual stimulation, as in the case of the thief who stole nothing but rubber mattresses from baby buggies in order to commit self-pollution (onanism) thereon. Clearer yet are the cases of pyromania, or firesetting for the purpose of experiencing sexual excitement, or even climax at the moment of firesetting, or while observing the flames shoot high, or while calling the fire department, or even while helping in extinguishing the blaze.

Similar incidents are known as to murder, assault, battery and other offenses against the person, committed by sadists (and sometimes willingly "suffered" by masochists!), and, indeed, perversity may run the entire gamut of the penal code. If offenses at all, that is, unless such perpetrators are exculpated under the law of "insanity," we must speak of them as sex offenses, but in the wider sense of that term. More properly, they are merely sexually motivated offenses, rather than true sex offenses. I shall not discuss them in this book.

But even within the sphere of sexual offenses in the narrower meaning of that term there exists a difficulty of

3

inclusion and exclusion. For example, abortion, in a sense, is a sex offense, but more frequently it is an aftermath of a sex offense. For surely, the fact that a manipulation takes place on the uterus (though not necessarily there) does not render it a sex offense. Hence, abortion has been excluded. Bigamy is also not covered, for while bigamy ordinarily is accompanied by sexual intercourse (and thus likely is adultery by at least one party) the reasons for a bigamous marriage are more often than not quite unrelated to sexual conduct. They tend to be of monetary nature.

Also omitted are such offenses as miscegenation (interracial marriage or intercourse) which is bound to disappear from the statute books in a very short time, as well as child concealing and similar offenses of a quasi-sexual nature. Nor have I gone into the problems of felony-murder, that is, a criminal liability for murder when in the course of a sexual offense (for example, rape or sodomy) a death results.

This leaves us with a wide variety of sexual offenses which are discussed in this book. Their classification is not an easy task. While in a general way they all protect the same interest, namely sexual purity or decency and morality (hence often the title: Offenses against morality and decency, in penal codes), each offense protects quite a distinct value. Take the crime of rape as an example. Principally the rape provisions protect the value of a woman's free choice as to when and with whom to engage in sexual relations. But the rape provisions are broad enough to cover also the protection of the sexual integrity of those who have no free choice, for example, feeble-minded women, or minors below the age of meaningful discretion. In short, the *specific* legally protected interest, or its antithesis, the harm which each offense entails, are not safe criteria for distinction among sexual offenses.

The mode of perpetration is a safer guide. Here we can clearly distinguish between sex offenses with heterosexual connexions, those with non-heterosexual connexions, and

4

those without any connexion. This classification has been adopted for this book.

Obviously, further distinctions must be made within each category to keep the various offenses apart; and I felt constrained to add two separate chapters, each one dealing with sexual offenses of a predominantly commercial nature, namely prostitution and obscenity.

The difficulty of classifying sexual offenses is increased by problems of legislative draftsmanship. Wide variations exist in the various states, though the principal practice is the infantile approach of simply classifying all offenses in alphabetical order. Even that is not without difficulties, because one and the same offense may be known by many different names. Moreover, in many states it has been customary to lump many sexual offenses in the same statutory provision. Where this has frustrated my scheme, the offenses have nevertheless been separated for purposes of compiling our tables.

Problems of statutory draftsmanship have been a source of constant irritation during the preparation of this book. Quite apart from the problems posed by illogical arrangements, awkward drafting frustrates an understanding of the law by lawyer and layman alike. Occasionally the drafting is so ridiculous that one gets the impression an analphabet drafted the sexual offense statutes. One example may suffice: For several generations, as a matter of fact until 1950, by awkward wording, the New York sodomy law seriously seemed to suggest the possibility of a bird making a sexual advance toward a human being, and the statute then humbly suggested that it would be a felony for the human being to yield to such an advance. My comment is simply that such a law was for the birds, and I am glad that finally, in the mid-20th century, an intelligent draftsman showed more sense than either the birds or his predecessor.

Chapter 1

ISSUES IN THE REGULATION OF
SEXUAL CONDUCT

The law operates with a very simple psychological theory, namely that of stimulus and response: The state uses punishment, or the threat thereof, to keep people from doing what they should not do. The premise is that the fear of unpleasant consequences governs most (but not all) of the people who are tempted to do forbidden things.

Mind you, for the vast majority of people as to the vast majority of forbidden things we do not have to threaten punishment. "Social" people simply will not kill or rape, because they know that such is harmful to society and to themselves. But some people just are not "social" and for most of these, so our experience shows, the threat of punishment works. We know this particularly from our experience with children, who are not yet social, and who are governed by the threat of punishment for naughty things—and reward for good deeds. Freud himself rested the structure of psychoanalysis on the fundament of this pain-pleasure principle.

Threat of Punishment

How effective is the threat of punishment? Until not too long ago it was believed that the more severe the possible punishment, the greater the effect. Today we know that this is not quite so. Of course, there must be some relation between the evil sought to be avoided and the measure of possible punishment. But much more than severity, it is the certainty that punishment will follow wrongdoing which governs the mind of the potential criminal.

In the sexual sphere it is virtually impossible to make for certainty of punishment, because most sexual misconduct is carried on by consenting parties in private. As a matter of fact, that goes for policy games or off-track betting. As to gambling, some eager law enforcement officers advocate widespread intrusion into the privacy of homes, by wiretaps, searches, etc. How else, they say, can we suppress those criminal offenses which are committed in privacy? The same argument goes for adultery, fornication, etc. Should we abandon the idea of the sanctity of the American home so as to increase our efficiency in suppressing adultery and fornication? These arguments are mainly designed to point to the dilemma in which we find ourselves today.

Because our detection efficiency as to most—but by no means all—sexual offenses is extremely low, the fear of punishment is not effective in influencing those to abstain from committing sexual offenses who have the inclination to commit them. This leaves us with an unenforced—and unenforceable—body of law on sexual offenses, and such may spell a grave danger to the very existence of our society.

Treason and the Sex Taboo

Historical research has shown that the oldest and most primitive societies always knew at least two legal prohibitions: one against treason and one against violating the sex taboo. These two prohibitions had to exist in order to preserve the very life of the society. To tamper with the nation's safety, or with its future—and a future there cannot be without normal sexual relations—has always been criminal, even when theft and mayhem were mere private wrongs. Next to the law of treason, then, the law of sexual offenses is of paramount importance to any society. It is quite true that both treason and sex crimes may be veiled

7

in mystical garbs. In primitive societies national safety and the sex taboo are usually dedicated to a special deity, and voilations of the rules are regarded as affronteries to this deity, and as bringing about the wrath of the deity. Today we have shed the garb of mysticism, but the rules have hardly changed, nor has their significance.

The details of our current law of sexual offenses were worked out in the late middle ages, and since shortly after this country had been settled, the law of sexual offenses underwent virtually no further change, except as to procedural details and punishments. But it is noteworthy that the official law of the government regulated only the smaller part of sexual conduct, and that the major part of sex offenses was subject to punishment by ecclesiastical or church courts. Since, however, no church courts ever existed in this country, the states themselves took over the function of punishing all forbidden sexual conduct.

There is reason to believe that the medieval law of sexual offenses did not correspond to the realities of sexual conduct among the population. Even at that time, then, the law pronounced an ideal situation, but one which it could not really bring about. To be quite sure, the mere fact that certain sexual practices were prohibited had its effect on the behavior of the people, more so, perhaps, than is true today, because somehow the law then was held in higher esteem than it is today, perhaps by reason of the attribution of divine origin to things legal in the middle ages. Sophisticated Americans of the 20th century no longer attribute divine qualities to their penal law, especially in view of the rather constant spectacle of legal changes which can be brought about in legislative halls, both through orderly political processes and through political horse trading.

The Fact of Unenforceability

But even though the attribution of divinity has vanished, the same substantive law of sexual offenses remains. Naturally, without the veil of divine sanction, the law of sexual offenses has lost much of its authority. Moreover, ever since the first two Kinsey reports—however much the ex-

8

perts are in disagreement about the reliability of the findings—revealed an incredibly wide gap between the law's expectations and the people's actual practices as to sexual conduct, the law of sexual offenses has lost its second major crutch: popular support.

The population flouts the law; it thereby indicates its dissatisfaction with it. A law without popular support cannot be effective. A law which does not enjoy the support of the majority is unfit for democratic society. Obviously, as to the latter point, it is also settled in democratic societies that a change must be brought about in an orderly manner, and not simply by disregard and disobedience. It remains to be seen whether the people, through their legislatures, are willing to bring the law into general accord with the practices they allow themselves. If the fate of reform bills in the legislatures of such key states as California and Illinois is any indication, it seems that the good people of these states, speaking through their legislatures, are as yet unwilling to grant sexual liberties to their neighbors which, at least according to Dr. Kinsey, they allow themselves.

Let us reiterate, then: there is absolutely no doubt that a wide gap exists between what our medieval law expects the public to do in the sexual sphere, and the actual practices of the public. Quite apart from the Kinsey reports, we need look only at the enormous discrepancy between the thousands of divorces ground out annually on the ground of adultery, and the handful of criminal prosecutions for that offense. Surely the discrepancy cannot be explained by the slight difference in proof! (Adultery for divorce need be proved only by clear, cogent and convincing evidence, but proof for an adultery conviction requires evidence beyond a reasonable doubt!)

Only an intellectually numb person can still maintain that the criminal law, with the traditional means at its command, can enforce the sexual standard which it endorses. It cannot, and we must face the fact.

But quite apart from its ineffectiveness, we may even attribute detrimental consequences to our current sex offender laws. Cases are not at all infrequent in which one partner to a homosexual relation will blackmail the other for years, threatening him with public prosecution unless he makes one payment after another to the blackmailer. Some psychiatrists even go as far as to say that the current rigid standards of our sex laws create unnecessary guilt feelings—resulting in neuroses—in many otherwise quite normal people who, apart from the violation of unrealistic laws, should not have guilt feelings.

Of course, this argument concedes that even the widely disrespected and disregarded sex law may have some impact on the human psyche. And if it is true that some—I suppose particularly sensitive—persons have guilt feelings, we must also concede a point to the opposition which claims that for many good citizens the mere fact that there is a law on the books constitutes a barrier. Indeed, some psychiatrists claim that this is a rather strong barrier and that repeal of the laws would remove the psychological block and open the floodgates to widespread profligacy. As always, both arguments cannot be verified by any qualitative or quantitative studies. That both arguments correctly describe the psychological facts as to some people, nobody can doubt.

Our discussion thus far has already acquainted us with the two principal means of regulation which the law employs: First, by merely pronouncing what is right and what is wrong, it sets the standards by which—it is hoped—most people will abide and, indeed, most people do. Let us call this *passive regulation*.

Second, by threatening negative consequences (punishment) for those who violate the standards, and by backing up the threat with execution of punishment, the law practices *active regulation*. Active regulation includes the individual reform efforts made on those who are in prison for the failure to comply, in the hope that ultimately they may be discharged as more law-abiding than they were before.

If now the evidence is mounting that passive regulation in the sexual sphere does not work properly, and that active

10

regulation is impossible of accomplishment, for evidentiary or other reasons, is our nation doomed to disintegrate in a cesspool of profligacy?

The Areas of Lesser Concern

Let us ask, then, whether we need be seriously concerned. Heretofore we have assumed that all sex laws are in existence to protect valid and significant values which are worthy of this protection and, which, indeed, are vital for the survival of our society. But when we now consider anthropological and biological evidence, we will soon learn that many of those values are not as vital as always assumed. Even if many of the communally (legally) disapproved sexual practices were to spread, no serious harm would result either to individuals or to society at large. (Note the emphasis on the word *many*.) It seems to me that the scales are now tipped in favor of reconsideration and modernization of our laws on sexual offenses. For whenever, in a democratic society, there is no real or threatened evil as the object of legislation, there simply should not be any law on the matter, especially if the law would be virtually unenforceable.

Lest there be any misunderstanding, I should make it quite clear that nobody in his right mind would propose the lifting of all legal restraints on sexual conduct. The debate centers solely on those sexual offenses which do not constitute a material harm and which, thus, are marked by these elements:

(1) Typically they are virtually impossible to detect with the ordinary methods of law enforcement.

(2) Experience has it that the criminal sanction is ineffective to prevent them.

(3) No physical force or violence is used, and no material hurt is inflicted.

(4) Both parties are consenting freely, and there is no abuse of confidence or relationship.

(5) The act is committed by adults, i.e., persons whose sexual patterns are established.

11

(6) The act is committed in private, so that no spread of the practice, especially to children, is conceivable.

(7) Because of this privacy, the public sentiment of decency is not outraged.

This would leave unaffected all sexual activities committed by force and violence and the infliction of hurt, those lacking consent, those committed on children or other dependent persons, or in public.

To be quite sure, by removing its criminal sanctions, the law could not make homosexual or otherwise perverse sexual activities "normal." The law would simply concede its inefficiency in promoting what some segments of society regard as normal, and it would, moreover, do what it always should do, that is, to withdraw modestly when there is no real or threatened harm which needs protection through the sharp weapons of the criminal law.

"Normal" Sexual Conduct

This raises the question as to what is normal sexual conduct. To the purist, the traditionalist, and perhaps the aesthetic person, normal sexual conduct is the genital connexion, through insertion of the male organ into the female organ, between married partners in private, until the emission of semen results, so that offspring may be procreated. It is this and virtually only this which the strict standard of morality permits.

And the law permits little more than this, i.e., it does permit the *coitus interruptus*, i.e., intercourse with disengagement prior to emission of semen, or other natural and sometimes artificial means of preventing conception. But there is absolutely no reason to believe that this minimum variety of sexual conduct also corresponds to the normal, and the Kinsey studies would certainly indicate otherwise. Indeed, biological, psychological and sociological evidence tends to refute the claim of normalcy which is made for the above mentioned narrow confines of marital sexual intercourse. But the point need receive no further consideration in this context because even if this were the limit of normalcy, it surely is not the function of the criminal law to prohibit everything which deviates from the norm.

Nor does the above definition exhaust the sphere of the "natural" in sexual relations. It is true that current law and morals regard every other sexual activity as unnatural. But surely this is unreal, for natural can be only that which is conditioned and determined by nature. Thus, if upon examining a man charged with sodomy (homosexual conduct) we find that the hormone structure of his body is predominantly female, although his physical appearance is predominantly male, it seems that his behavior was rather natural, namely in accordance with his natural endowment. These cases are not frequent, but they do occur. It is seriously questioned, therefore, whether current definitions of "the natural" are in accordance with reality, and whether the law should continue to regard what it thinks to be abnormal as also implicity unnatural.

It may be contended that the line of my argument will sanction every rape or lust murder as long as the defendant proves that he suffered from some abnormality and that it was this abnormality which "naturally" led to his abnormal, but natural, offensive sexual expression. The answer is simple: In the first place, I would require—and the law does require—a strict cause and effect relationship for any abnormality to be considered; in the second place, the mere fact that some people, by nature, cannot respond to the expectations of some sex laws, does not necessitate the repeal of all sex laws. In the third place, repeal of innocuous laws is not at all inconsistent with the retention of beneficial laws.

But there do remain some human beings who simply cannot comply with the law. If the reasons for such non-compliance are beyond their control, the criminal law will not, and cannot, punish. Such has always been the rule and will continue to be so. Obviously, this does not mean that dangerous sexual attackers will be permitted to roam the streets. It simply means that some other branch of the law, the mental health law for example, must do the job which is beyond the reach of the criminal law. But this

13

matter is best discussed under the heading Sexual Conduct and Mental Abnormality, below.

The propositions which are here advanced are by no means novel. A long line of reform commissions, studies, institutes, publications and individual scholars has made these points before. Quite recently England has taken serious steps in the direction of a realistic overhauling of its sex offender laws. And the highly reputed American Law Institute strongly advocates a modernization along the lines here indicated. Indeed, there is a world-wide trend in this direction, the beginnings of which I traced many years ago for the Sex Offenders Commission for the State of Illinois and which now has received a most powerful expression through a resolution of the Fourth International Congress of Criminology in the Netherlands, in 1960. This Congress endorsed a realistic approach to matters of sexual offenses for all the world. Years and decades are expected to pass before the new policy will trickle from the lofty heights of the research and academic level to practical implementation in the courts. The mill of the law grinds slowly, but the change will surely come.

This development is a tremendously important one, for it is the emancipation of mankind from the last remaining superstitions. Thistles will not grow where the seed of Onan falls. Nothing, simply nothing will grow there. We need not fear destruction of the nation through sin, debauch, and insanity if married couples exceed the bounds of what is presently regarded as lawful intercourse. Nobody could express the thought better than a fellow member of the long extinct Illinois Sex Offenders Commission, the late Dr. Alfred C. Kinsey who, at an enclave of scientific committee members, exclaimed to several of us: *The Criminal Law's dictatorial power must end at the bedroom door* —and I should like to add: *and at the barn door*.

But once again, I know of no academic member of the modern school who would contend that the removal of a criminal sanction renders such conduct either desirable or moral. The law simply cannot direct itself against all immorality, and the judgment as to what is moral must be

14

entrusted to the responsible human being, who must engage in his own soul searching with the help of those spiritual agencies whose principal function is the support of the moral standard. If we read in the New Testament: "Clean first the inside of the cup and the dish that the outside may be clean," we find here an appeal to those agencies which can reach the inside. The law is ill-equipped to do so. But that both the inside and the outside of man should be clean, no one will question.

Chapter 2

MENTAL STATE AS AN ELEMENT
IN SEXUAL OFFENSES

The threats of the criminal law are not directed at all people. In fact, they can be directed only at relatively normal, rational or healthy people, that is, at responsible people. The criminal law has always excluded from its sweep those people who cannot possibly be expected to be influenced by the law's command. This holds true for the sphere of the sexual.

A human vegetable with such a low I.Q. that he cannot possibly understand the words of a legal or moral command, cannot possibly be expected to behave accordingly. The mentally disturbed person who lives in an unreal world of ghosts and devils and witches, cannot be expected to sense reality when it comes to commands as to sexual conduct. I remember a mental patient (Miss F), a once beautiful and still young lady, the daughter of a noted scholar, whose sense of reality was completely lost in the grip of schizophrenia, and who engaged in constant self-satisfaction, regardless of her surroundings or the presence of others. Obviously, the standards of morals and law meant nothing to her. The threat of punishment for her misconduct is fruitless; punishment would be absurd.

The general rules of the so-called law of insanity (a misnomer) also apply to persons charged with sexual offenses. These rules differ from state to state, and their interpretation varies even among courts of the same state. Many courts apply the traditional Anglo-American "insanity" test, which rests on the accumulated wisdom of the ages, but they do so without any imagination and insight into the meaning of the test and its purpose. Such courts will satisfy themselves with an answer to the question whether the defendant knew the difference between right and wrong, and a "surface" knowledge on the level of verbal response will suffice. This is a complete misunderstanding; it is false and erroneous, and no amount of repetition of the mistake can set it right. If properly understood by the judiciary, the currently prevailing test of insanity would exempt from punishment anybody who by nature, that is through mental or emotional disease or defect, is incapable of committing a crime, however much destruction and harm such a person may be able to wreak.

Each crime consists of two aspects. The first aspect is always rational human conduct. Thus a person who has no meaningful conception of what he is doing or, perhaps, he whose behavior is the result of psychic forces and emotional processes beyond his control, is not engaged in rational human conduct. His activity may be *mere* irrational behavior; it may be convulsion or spasm; but it is not conduct or an *act* in the legal sense. In short, anyone who has no meaningful conception of what he is doing, is not engaged in a rational human act and thus cannot incur criminal liability.

The second aspect of each crime is always the knowledge of wrongdoing. This is an important demand of the criminal law, for surely, nobody can be expected to abstain from wrongdoing unless he knows that what he proposes to do is wrong. Thus, a mentally ill woman (Miss G) who is under the impression that the Lord has commanded her to have sexual intercourse with the Saviour, and who believes that her bearded companion is the Saviour, cannot possibly be punished for fornication. In short, nobody can be punished unless he or she understands that what he or she is doing is wrong.

But it is important to remember that in all such cases the inability to engage in rational conduct, or to realize one's wrongdoing, must be attributable to a mental illness,

17

or a mental defect or abnormality. And we must always keep in mind that the test is more strict in some states than it is in others, and that some judges and courts simply have more wisdom than others.

The law of "insanity" is difficult enough in ordinary criminal cases. In the sphere of sexual offenses it is particularly difficult. Here, more than in any other sphere of penal law, the most fantastic claims are made to the effect that everybody who commits a sexual offense is *ipso facto* "insane." After what I have said about the standards of normalcy, and as to what is natural, this does not at all follow.

But I must make an important concession. Our statute books contain some prohibitions which describe conduct so clearly indicative of the mental abnormality of the perpetrator, as to draw the very purpose of the law in question. For example, the law threatens long terms of imprisonment for intercourse with a corpse. I simply cannot conceive of a psychiatrist who would succeed in this second half of the twentieth century in establishing that a person who engages in such conduct is perfectly mentally healthy. Indeed, no behavior can better illustrate a symptom of the loss of a meaningful conception of one's behavior or of a sense of right and wrong, as such fantastically perverse conduct as that. There is absolutely no justification for continuing such offenses on the statute books. Such matters must be taken care of by the mental health laws, but not by criminal law.

And I must make a second concession to the psychiatrists. In the sphere of sexual offenses they have succeeded more than elsewhere in demonstrating the background of deviancy, the principal reason being, I suppose, that psychiatrists have shown more interest in sexual than in nonsexual deviancy.

The factors which go into the makeup of sexual misbehavior frequently emanate from the deepest recesses of the human psyche. Nevertheless, frequently the misbehavior would not have occurred, if only Mr. X, or whoever he might be, also had had a normal, social, well-developed conscience to counteract his anti-social (perhaps unrecognized) sexual desires. Traditionally, the law will impose liability in such cases, if for no other reason than to subject that person to a process of re-socialization, in other words, to subject him to an experience which is meant to make him stronger against temptation than he was before, or—in psychiatric terms—to strengthen his superego.

That the effort frequently fails is not due to a failure of theory but, more frequently, due to a failure adequately to implement the theory in practice: There just are not enough trained people around to do the re-socializing!

But responsiveness to the psychological stimuli of the law, and thus, legal responsibility, is not a matter of yes or no. It is measurable only on a sliding scale. Between the female patient I have described above (Miss F) and Mr. Y, who is a perfect master over his actions and who violates the law only if this derives to his pleasure without the least danger of detriment, there are many shadings of responsiveness. Mr. X is certainly not identical with Mr. Y, though Y stands closer to X than the Misses F and G, who are likewise not identical. Between the relatively clear cases of F and G on the one hand, and X and Y on the other, there is the twilight zone of the "partial responders," or the slow responders.

From my student days in a seminar on forensic psychiatry I remember that an old man—let us call him Mr. P —was "demonstrated" to us. Mr. P was a pedophiliac, i.e., a person who fondles and sexually molests little children. Apart from this deviancy Mr. P was perfectly harmless. He was quite well known to the police in the neighborhood in which he resided, and as soon as, feeling unobserved, he started attracting little children with candy or toys, they would haul him to the station house and charge him as a vagrant. He had undergone many treatment experiments at the psychiatric university clinic, yet without success. The criminal law's threat of sanction meant little to him. The rigid standard of the insanity test could not exculpate him. Fortunately, in that jurisdiction, the law gave special recognition to those who are not completely "insane"—as I have defined that standard above,—but who are largely, *though surely not fully,* "normal." Certainly, Mr. P cannot be blamed as much for his act as Mr. Y, nor can he be exculpated like the Misses F and G. Treatment in such cases will ordinarily do more good than punishment, although treatment is necessarily subject to restraint, and that may be punishment enough. But, as in the case of Mr. P, psychiatry may not know—yet!—how to cure. And then the law is confronted with the awkward choice either to detain such a person for life, or to leave him at large, well knowing that he will continue to make a nuisance of himself!

Chapter 3

CRIMINALIZATION OF SEXUAL CONDUCT

On principle, if such a person really is a mere nuisance, it may be preferable to leave him at large, subject to supervision, or at least the attention of the authorities. In more dangerous cases, or even if there is any doubt, such a person must be detained, though primarily under the aegis of the mental health law.

Non-Criminal Sanctions

In many states the legislatures have specifically provided for such cases. Special laws have been enacted, usually under the title "Criminal Sexual Psychopath Law," in order to commit all those sexual offenders to institutions "until cured" who, if at large, would constitute a danger to themselves or others. As a practical matter, these laws are rarely employed, because the remedy is so extremely drastic, even though such confinement is not regarded as a punishment. It is meant to be a mere protective device. Naturally, it is a protective device which is employed very much against the defendant's wishes and occasionally even without the ordinary protections of a truly criminal process.

The infrequency of application of these laws is explainable in part by the reluctance of psychiatrists to virtually condemn people for life—for the psychiatric report is the *sine qua non* for such commitments—especially since many, if not most, of the offenders who fall under such laws are but mere minor nuisances. But there are three other factors which enter the picture: first, it has long been established by criminologists that sexual offenders do not, ordinarily, progress from minor criminality to major criminality, as is the case with thieves and robbers. Rather, their patterns are pretty well confined to a given sphere of conduct. Hence, there is no grave reason to fear worse from a given sexual offender, and he is thus not confined for life.

Second, the number of really dangerous and violent sexual offenders is extremely small. At the most it amounts to 5% of all those who are charged with sexual offenses. Third, as to sexual offenders who do not suffer from a behavioral disorder (as did our Mr. P), the recidivism rate is extremely low. In other words, a normal (non-psychopathological) violater of the sex laws is more likely to learn his lesson from punishment than most other types of criminals. Hence, in such cases, the so-called criminal sexual psychopath statutes are not needed.

There is at least one other non-criminal remedy available for sex offenders in some states, and that is castration. According to reports from the Netherlands and Denmark, the results of castration performed on sexual offenders are extremely good. The theory simply is that such a surgical remedy will remove the urge which led to the offense.

The experiences in this country have been otherwise. Quite apart from distaste for such a non-reversible remedy in this country—even when the subject consents—the results in the few states which have experimented with that practice have not proven it to be more successful than other less distasteful forms of treatment. It is true that there have been successful cases, but there is no evidence to indicate that these offenders would not have reformed anyway (as many do!), and many cases had no beneficial effect at all. I am reminded of a case reported from California in which an operation performed on a rapist was successful enough to keep him from committing further rapes—but he turned to molesting little children and murder!

Criminal Sanctions

We can now turn to the more conventional sanctions of the sex offender statutes. These are the criminal sanctions, or punishments proper. It cannot be my purpose to discuss in this connection the theories and practices of punishment. Suffice it to say that what is true for other forms of criminality, insofar as punishment is concerned, is equally true of sex offenses. Our tables indicate the specific maximum punishments provided for each offense or group of offenses in a given state, specially mentioning the increased punishment for repeated offenses and offenses committed under aggravating circumstances.

Many statutes provide for fines in addition to imprisonment or in the alternative, and in many states collateral punishments or detriments are specifically provided in the sex offense laws, e.g., loss of liquor license, fingerprinting, etc. Many more states than those specifically mentioned provide for fingerprinting—which, after all, is an onerous burden, effective for the rest of one's life—or loss of licenses. But in such cases the remedy is provided by general laws, which we have not incorporated, rather than by the specific laws on sexual offenses.

Particularly noteworthy are the wide discrepancies in the punishments provided by the laws of the various states. What in one state may be subject to a minor jail sentence or a fine, in another state may be subject to long term imprisonment at hard labor. There surely is no justification for such gross inconsistencies in a relatively unitary nation as ours. It is to be hoped that such inequalities will be weeded out in the sweep of legislative reforms now underfoot in many states

Applicability of the General Doctrines of Criminal Law

Just as the criminal law's doctrine of insanity is applicable to sex offenders as much as to all other offenders, all the other doctrines of criminal law are applicable, too. I can here do no more than point to a few of the more important doctrines and simply state their scope:

ATTEMPTS: The average crime on the books is meant to prevent a specific harm from resulting, for example, forceful intercourse with an unwilling woman. As to most such crimes, the law regards the protected interest (the female sexual integrity) so high, that it threatens punishment even for the mere attempt to commit the principal crime, rape. Therefore, one who tries to rape a woman, is punishable for an attempt to rape, even if he is unsuccessful in his efforts, for example, where he is surprised by witnesses, or where his attacks have been thwarted by the woman's defenses.

A criminal attempt may be defined as an act directed at completion of a crime, but failing to accomplish it by reason of factual obstacles or abandonment. The law of attempt is wrought with great difficulties and any generalization here offered must be taken with care. Simply by way of illustration, there is one difficulty encountered under the law of New York which defines an attempt as an "act, done with intent to commit a crime, and tending but failing to effect its commission." (§ 2.2, N.Y.P.L.) Under this statute it has been held that where the defendant thought he was successfully committing a crime, but where, unbeknown to him, the facts were such that he could never succeed in accomplishing what the statute prohibited, he was not guilty of a criminal attempt. I should like to venture this example: If the defendant thinks he is committing the crime of statutory rape, because he believes the girl to be fifteen years of age, he will never succeed in violating the statutory rape law when in fact the girl is nineteen years old; nor is he even guilty of trying to violate the law. (A corollary to this case will be discussed under "Ignorance of Law," *infra.*)

Some attempts have long gained independent significance. Thus, an "indecent assault" is really nothing but an attempted indecent physical contact—which would include rape—and conceivably, a defendant could be charged with both an indecent assault and an attempted rape. The scope of proof differs but slightly.

In our tables we have made no provision for a collection

of sexual assault statutes, nor have we specifically mentioned the punishment for attempts, which are usually lower. Rather, since I regard assaults as merely substantivized attempts of a greater crime, or at least as something preliminary to an envisaged greater crime, special statutory provisions for sexual assaults are mentioned in the tables for those crimes to which the assault is the preliminary. For example, assaults with intent to rape are mentioned in the tables on Rape; ordinary indecent assaults are listed in the table on Indecent Liberties.

Some legally protected interests, such as sexual purity and morality, are held in such high esteem by the law that even specific acts which merely endanger (as distinguished from actually destroy or damage) the interest, are made punishable by law. Here we are invading the sphere of *preparatory acts* which have been made independent offenses. To be quite sure, ordinarily a merely endangering or preparatory act is not criminal, unless amounting to an attempt. But some specific endangering or preparatory acts have been made criminal. Examples are the transportation of female persons in interstate commerce for the purpose of prostitution, debauchery or any other immoral purpose. Here we see that the transportation preparatory to the real violation of decency and morality, i.e., a preparatory act, was made criminal. Or the sale of alluring literature, prohibited by law, may be regarded as merely preparatory to sexual offenses committed as a result of being "allured." On the other hand, the sale of such literature itself may be regarded as a violation of decency, and then the prohibited manufacture or importation of such literature is the preparatory or endangering activity.

The question then arises, how far can the legislature go back in conceivable causal chains in order to protect the members of the public from direct harms in the sexual sphere? The answer lies in various relatively vague, constitutional provisions, and the court's standards are rather vague as well, in terms of "real harms," "actual or clearly threatened" danger, "immediate connection between the matter prohibited and the evil sought to be avoided," and so on. Just as one cannot possibly insure himself against all casualties, the law cannot protect the citizen against all remote dangers. But in this sphere we can spot the real difference between liberal and patriarchal society. Liberal society will leave the general public to guard themselves as much as possible; patriarchal society will likely prohibit kissing and flirting because it may result in sexual outrages.

ACCESSORYSHIP: In most sex offenses — as in most crimes—there is a perpetrator and a victim (besides society itself as a victim), as for example in rape, where we have the (male) rapist and the (female) victim. In some crimes there is only a perpetrator and no *actual* victim, though the law may construe a given person to be the victim, as in White Slave Traffic Act violations, in which the transported female person is regarded as the victim, however willing she may have been. And that probably goes for indecent exposure, where the "victims," the spectators, conceivably were rather willing.

This distinction between perpetrator and victim simply implies that only one of the two, namely the perpetrator, can be punished, and the victim not. Such is the situation in White Slave Traffic Act violations as much as in indecent exposure, because in one case the transported person and in the other case the spectator cannot be punished under the laws under which the actual perpetrator is punished, although in both cases the "victims" may be punishable under different provisions. For example, the transported prostitute may be guilty of prostitution, the spectator at a lewd show may be punishable for loitering.

But in many sex offenses we have no human victims in any sense of that term. Think of bestiality (the connexion of man and beast).Unless one wants to regard the beast as the victim, the crime consists solely of the act of one person. I was rather amused by the proposal of an Austrian law reformer who truly thought of the beast as a victim, and proposed to stiffen the punishments for cruelty to animals, also proposing to drop bestiality from the statute book.

Many sexual offenses require several guilty perpetrators, for example, sodomy in many forms. Both the active and

26

the passive participant to an unnatural sexual connexion could be equally guilty of the crime, as principals, or principals in the first degree. If they had posted a guard at the door to warn of oncoming visitors, the guard, if he acted knowingly, would be guilty as a principal in the second degree or, as he is sometimes called, an aider and abettor or accessory (actually or constructively) *at* the fact. All these parties are equally punishable in all states, although as a practical matter, the actual principals would probably receive a stiffer punishment for their greater guilt than the lookout, or accessory at the fact. These parties must be distinguished from the accessory before the fact, for example the landlady who knowingly made the room available for the commission of the offense or who instigated or helped before the fact in any way to the actual commission of the crime subsequently committed, or at least of an attempt to do so. Many states have abolished all these distinctions and punish all parties equally.

Lastly, I should mention the accessory after the fact, who in all states is still regarded as a separate entity. He is the person who in any way knowingly helps actively to conceal the crime or its perpetrators, after its commission.

There is still a different form of participation, namely the conspiracy, but the rules as to conspiracy are too technical for discussion in this context. Moreover, conspiracy charges in sexual offenses are rather rare, except perhaps in Mann Act violations, or under the prostitution statutes.

Difficulties arise when the law posits that the perpetrator must have a certain status or character, and the accessory lacks this status or character, or vice versa. Consider the case of a husband (Mr. Q) who aids in the commission of a rape by another (Mr. R) of his wife (Mrs. Q). Clearly Mr. R is guilty of rape. But is Mr. Q guilty as an accessory? Husbands cannot rape their wives—by the better authority. But by the prevailing opinion, Mr. Q would here be guilty of rape of his own wife, as an accessory.

MERGER AND CONCURRENCE OF OFFENSES: The same act may violate several laws. Thus, when a father has intercourse with his minor daughter, he is guilty of both incest and statutory rape and he may be properly convicted of both. Whenever there is lacking identity in one or more respects of the two or more offenses charged to have been committed by the same act, there may be a conviction of both. Incest calls for proof of family relationship, but not for any age limit, statutory rape calls for proof of an age limit, but not for any family relationship.

Some sexual offenses, however, are completely merged in others. For example, the crime of rape (forceful intercourse) necessarily includes an [indecent] assault. Depending on how the jury views the evidence, it may convict of either rape, or the lesser included offense of indecent assault, but not of both offenses simultaneously, because a rape conviction necessarily includes all the elements of an indecent assault.

Occasionally it is difficult to decide whether one and the same conduct pattern constitutes one or several commissions of the same offense. This is an important question, because the punishment will be multiplied if several offenses have been committed. By way of example, in a Florida case the defendant fondled the thirteen year old victim in a lewd and lascivious manner at least twice on the same day. The Florida Supreme Court reversed the case for a factual determination as to whether this was one continuous act, or whether there were two separated occurrences. This is the proper solution.

Lastly, I should like to call attention to the fact that the same ·act may conceivably violate the law of two sovereigns, namely the state government and the federal government. Until recently in such cases two trials and two convictions would most certainly follow, but the practice has been changed lately.

IGNORANCE AND ERROR: Suppose a man, sporting a beautiful looking Mexican divorce document, engages in sexual intercourse with another woman. Very much to his surprise he is arrested for adultery and is told that his Mexican divorce decree is worth no more than the paper and the printer's ink thereon (as is usually the case!). He did not know the law (of divorce), and indeed, he shares this ignorance with many courts and attorneys.

A similar case would be that of the defendant who has intercourse with a seventeen year old girl because he is under the impression that the age limit of consent to intercourse lies at sixteen. In fact, in the particular state, it may lie at eighteen. Or suppose that two lesbians from Germany, where female homosexuality is not prohibited, engage in lesbian relations in this country, and to their surprise they are charged with sodomy.

These are cases of ignorance, or error, of law, and the answer almost universally given by the courts is that such ignorance does not excuse. Among the scholars of criminal law there has been a lively rebellion against this doctrine, on utilitarian and moral grounds, but so far with little success in the courts.

Contrary to this rule, the rule with respect to error or ignorance of fact, is otherwise. A reasonable and excusable, non-negligent and *bona fide* (good faith) ignorance or mistake of fact which prevents the defendant from realizing the specific unlawfulness of his conduct, is a good defense.

But the exceptions to this rule are noteworthy, especially for sexual offenses. Most courts will hold that ignorance of weakmindedness of the woman is no defense to a charge of rape of a weakminded woman, or that ignorance of the minority of the girl is no defense to the charge of statutory rape, or even that ignorance of family relationship is no defense to a charge of incest, etc. The reason assigned for such a harsh rule is that the defendant was doing something indecent anyway (illicit intercourse) and that he should therefore be blamed for all the unknown consequences. This rule is hideous, and a number of courts have refused to apply it in its rigor. Obviously, there is a great difference in terms of illegality, immorality and actual guilt, between a relatively innocuous intercourse on the one hand and a heinous incestual relationship, or rape-like intercourse on the other. It is to be hoped that the law will undergo a gradual change in this respect.

Chapter 4

RAPE

Forcible Rape

Rape may be defined as an act of enforced, or forceful, sexual intercourse ("carnal knowledge") of a woman, without her consent. The perpetrator, thus, is male, the victim female. "Carnal knowledge" requires a penetration of the penis into the vagina, however slight, but emission of semen is not required. The force must be such as to overcome the resistance of the victim, and if the resistance is half-hearted, the law is likely to draw an inference of consent. Hence, the law requires both actual physical force on the part of the perpetrator and lack of consent, with evidence thereof, (usually through the utmost resistance possible under the circumstances), on the part of the victim. Obviously, the circumstances must be considered. It would be unrealistic to expect the victim to make a violent defense when a revolver is pointed at her temple. In view of the rule that consent and rape are inconsistent, it has occasionally been claimed by defense attorneys that unless the victim ultimately does consent after all, no intercourse could have taken place. But the law stands firm, that submission to superior force is not tantamount to consent. It may be assent—for fear of death or serious bodily harm—and such assent on the part of the victim is consistent with a rape conviction.

This opens the issue of the reality of consent. The distinction between *consent* and *assent* points to a peculiar difficulty. Assent and consent are distinguishable only by the inducement. A failure to object, on the part of the victim, would amount to consent, if the victim is a sane and sound person. But what if the victim is feebleminded, or defrauded into believing that she is married, or drugged, or under age and thus cannot give a legally relevant consent? The courts have given these answers:

Some courts have said that the "consent" of a female person legally incapable of consenting is no consent; at most it is assent. But while a few courts have now concluded that for want of the element of force, no *rape* conviction can be found, others have supplied force by fiction: Every intercourse requires force in the sense of physical exertion. Hence, the crime of rape is complete in such instances. This is indeed fictitious, and the older authorities never would have satisfied themselves with normal sexual physical exertion as "force."

Indeed, most states found it necessary to enlarge the coverage of the crime of rape so as to make it rape for a man to have intercourse with a woman whose consent was obtained by any sort of fraud (a few statutes have been interpreted more restrictively, as requiring fraud as to the very nature of the act), or with a feebleminded or drugged woman. This simply amounts to an abandonment of the element of force in such cases.

In all states rape is an offense of the most serious type, a felony, with provision for long terms of imprisonment. In some states it is even a capital crime.

It has been a long-standing proposition in the law that a man could not legally commit rape upon his wife. Indeed, for centuries most societies viewed wives as their husbands' property, and in 47 of the United States, even today, a man cannot be prosecuted for compelling his wife to have sexual intercourse. Oregon is one of the exceptions. In 1977, a new state law eliminating marital privilege and cohabitation as defenses against charges of rape was passed. At the time of publication of this edition in early 1979, arguments and testimony were being heard in the nation's first criminal prosecution of a husband alleged to have raped his wife while they were

31

living together. This case will probably go through the appeals route regardless of the verdict. Iowa, Delaware and New Jersey have rape laws similar to the Oregon statute. We would predict here that under the continuing influence and pressure from feminists, libertarians, and legal scholars, the number of jurisdictions embracing this kind of legislation will increase and that constitutional tests on appeal will uphold their constitutionality.

In any event, a divorced or legally separated woman can be raped in the legal sense by her husband. A forcible sexual attack that meets all the other criteria for rape would not fall outside the definition because of their former relationship.

A model statute on rape and related offenses (including definitions of the relevant terms) has been proposed by the American Law Institute:

Section 213.1 Rape and Related Offenses
 (1) Rape. *A male who has sexual intercourse with a female not his wife is guilty of rape if:*
 (a) he compels her to submit by force or by threat of imminent death, serious bodily injury, extreme pain or kidnapping, to be inflicted on anyone; or
 (b) he has substantially impaired her power to appraise or control her conduct by administering or employing without her knowledge drugs, intoxicants or other means for the purpose of preventing resistance; or
 (c) the female is unconscious; or
 (d) the female is less than 10 years old.

Rape is a felony of the second degree unless (i) in the course thereof the actor inflicts serious bodily injury upon anyone, or (ii) the victim was not a voluntary social companion of the actor upon the occasion of the crime and had not previously permitted him sexual liberties, in which cases the offense is a felony of the first degree. Sexual intercourse includes intercourse per os or per annum, with some penetration however slight, emission is not required.

(3) Gross Sexual Imposition. A male who has sexual intercourse with a female not his wife commits a felony of the third degree if:
 (a) he compels her to submit by any threat that would

prevent resistance by a woman of ordinary resolution;
or
(b) he knows that she suffers from a mental disease or
defect which renders her incapable of appraising the
nature of her conduct; or
(c) he knows that she is unaware that a sexual act is
being committed upon her or that she submits because
she falsely supposes that he is her husband.

Distortions of rape statistics have declined largely as a result of changing sex mores, improved crime reporting, and feminists' efforts to persuade victims to go to the police. Virginity is no longer so greatly valued, so that a woman who has been raped by a stranger is more likely to report this fact. An important development has been the work of feminists who have worked with police officers (male and female) to make them more sympathetic to complainants. They have set up specialized police rape units and treatment centers and have instituted other mechanisms for giving assistance to victims.

Forcible rapes in the United States have increased by 48 percent from 1970 to 1975. The rate of victimization (number of victims per 100,000 inhabitants) rose during this period by 41 percent. Over the same period, all violent crimes increased by 39 percent, the rate by 32 percent; all "index crimes" (seven major crimes for which reliable figures are believed to be available and that are used as an index of serious criminality) went up by 39 percent, the rate by 33 percent. These figures suggest that the increase in rape has been real, not an artificial side effect of the woman's liberation movement, which has encouraged reporting. One can therefore also conclude that America is faced with a rising wave of violence and crime and not so much with a specific rape epidemic.

The traditional rape case usually involves two witnesses-the male defendant and the female victim. While courts deal with homosexual rape cases, the overwhelming majority are heterosexual. In most cases the only prosecution witness to the crime is the female victim. Thus the trial becomes a credibility battle between the female victim and the male defendant. Two issues have to be decided by the jury: whether the intercourse has occurred and whether the sex act was committed against the

33

will of the victim. Since what is involved here is a credibility contest the defense attorney employs every lawful strategy to discredit the female history of the victim to show that she is immoral or promiscuous. The second tactic is the invocation of a "cautionary instruction." The law in most states requires the judge to instruct the jury at the close of the case to "examine the testimony of the complaining witness with caution." The testimony of other witnesses is not to be considered this way.

In recent years, legislation has been introduced in many states to shift the focus of rape cases from victim to defendant. More than a third of the states have enacted laws prohibiting use of cautionary instructions and the cross-examination of the rape victim about her past sexual conduct. Thus the assumption that if the victim is of unchaste character it is likely that she consented on this particular occasion no longer prevails. This has resulted in greater number of convictions of defendants who formerly managed to get away with their crime.

For the discussion of statutory rape, see the section on this topic in Chapter VII, *Sexual Offenses Against Children and Minors*. It would be appropriate, however, to make a number of comments on certain aspects of this topic within this chapter dealing with rape. The crucial distinction between forcible rape and statutory rape in terms of the defendant, is that because of age of consent is the critical factor, not the willingness of the younger partner, the previous chastity of the female is legally not relevant although many judges take it into account as a mitigating factor in determining the punishment to be imposed on the male (if the victim was a child and not a teenager, no consideration at all is accorded the male). It should be understood, in any case, that a woman's previous promiscuity is not a defense in the former situations, it is introduced to a attempt to show that the defendant would not need to use force and in fact did not do so.

Adultery & Fornication

As simple as the notion of adultery is for the divorce court, so much the more difficult it is for the criminal court. There is absolutely no agreement among the various states, the reason being that the common law of England did not bother about the offense, and American statutes and judges borrowed their definitions from a variety of sources. In a general way it is true that adultery is the unlawful and voluntary sexual intercourse between a man and a woman, at least one of whom is married to a third party. This definition puts the strain on the word "unlawful." Some courts have said that the act is unlawful only when committed openly and notoriously or lewdly, or that it is unlawful only for the married party, and a few have restricted it even to the woman, provided she is the one who has a spouse. In any event, the party who under these definitions goes free of adultery might nevertheless be punished, but his or her crime has a different name (fornication, discussed below).

Since, fornication, a clandestine act of sexual intercourse between two adult unmarried persons has generally not been deemed to be a crime at common law, a specific statute is necessary to make this widespread activity criminal. In at least ten states there is no such statute. Men and women may copulate in these jurisdictions if they are of full age and if neither force nor money is involved without fear of policemen, courts, or jailers. As one state court put it, "Voluntary sexual intercourse between a man and a woman, both being unmarried, is not a stautory offense, but is merely a meretricious transaction."

Adultery, however, is far more universally condemned. There are only five states, Arkansas, Louisiana, Nevada, New Mexico, and Tennessee, which do not prohibit adultery by means of criminal penalties, as against ten states that do not forbid fornication. New York state, for example, has no statute directed against fornication. But this same state makes adultery a misdemeanor punishable by six months' imprisonment and/or a $250 fine. Adultery is regarded more seriously than fornication because of its treat to the family, hence it is almost a universal ground for divorce.

Many fornication and adultery statutes are not violated by a single act of sexual intercourse between two adults not married

35

to each other. These so-called "lewd and lascivious cohabitation" statutes require such elements as "living together in adultery or fornication," living in a state of cohabitation," "living in open and notorious adultery," "cohabitation together as husband and wife without being married," before a penal offense is committed.

Adultery is not always a secret act. It is sometimes committed with full knowledge of the adulterer's spouse. In some cases both husband and wife are engaging in sex acts with other partners, with each other's approval, even assistance. During the countercultural movements of the 1960's, group sex and mate swapping were carried out by a considerable minority of the population, according to the estimates of some social scientists. By the mid-1970's it was said that "swinging" was on the decline, assuming it was ever as widely practiced as the media and social scientists of "relevancy" led the public to believe.

Legal sanctions against adulterers, including "swappers," are rarely exercised. Swappers, however, may be sometimes harrassed for lewd and lascivious conduct or under some other catchall sex statute. The Model Penal Code of the American Law Institute proposes that adulterous relations not be illegal.

The law against fornication, when it has not been repealed, has fallen into decline, withering away under the impact of mass open defiance, lack of prosecution and enforcement, a complete absence of public support, and apathy toward the law (including ignorance of the law) on the part of violators.

Not only are laws repealed or forgotten, they are sometimes "amended" by new court interpretations. So it has been with fornication. In many jurisdictions, statutes have been interpreted as referring only to open cohabitation, and in others the law has been invoked only against interracial couples. It is generally agreed, even by supporters of a traditional morality and a nonpermissive if not a repressive sexuality, that fornication is not the business of the law. Whether the law should even permit discrimination against fornicators on the part of employers, educational institutions and others is a related matter.

Summary, then, punishment for those found guilty of fornication, often the same as that for adultery, has ranged from small fines to several months' imprisonment. In Utah, a maximum sentence of six months in jail is prescribed. In addition to laws that have been applicable only in cases of open cohabitation, many state laws under fornication statutes specifically aplied only in instances of miscegenation (such laws have been held unconstitutional and are no longer in effect in the United States). Finally, some laws were held to apply only if the couple registered falsely in a hotel as man and wife. The Model Penal Code of the American Law Institute dropped all penalties for adult nonmarital sexual behavior, as was done by Illinois, New York, and several other states during the years following World War II.

Lewd Cohabition

With the offense of lewd cohabitation we are entering an area of even greater multifariousness of definitions. As the term implies, states which have such statutes would require "cohabitation" between a man and a woman, so that a lewd or indecent act of a single person would not qualify under such a statute, although the lewdness of single persons, or the lewdness of couples without cohabitation, may be punishable under separate statutes.

But there is no agreement among the states as to what constitutes lewd cohabitation. Some states require an act of intercourse, others simply a living together regardless of intercourse, others yet a living together with intercourse. But in any event, such cohabitation must be lewd or "lascivious," and this requires an offensiveness of a sexual nature.

There are some noteworthy statutory qualifications which must be met in order to have this offense constituted. In some states, for example, the relationship covered must be miscegenous (inter-racial). Without going too far out on a limb, I should hazard the guess that before long the qualifications as to miscegenation will be removed as unconstitutional. The penalties for this offense are usually slight. It is customarily a misdemeanor, though not universally so. Very frequently the punishments are identical to those provided for fornication.

Seduction and Abduction

Seduction, so easily confused with abduction, is a statutory offense without a basis in the common law. Hence, its meaning in this country is dependent on widely diverging statutes.

The crime of seduction exists principally for the protection of a weakness which the legislator assumes to exist, especially in young (some statutes have upper age limits) or unmarried female persons. While an act of intercourse with such a person—other factors being absent—alone may be nothing worse than fornication, in seduction the surrender of the body (in some states: the surrender of chastity), must be achieved by artifice, strategem, trickery and deceit, or a promise of marriage and in some states solely by the latter.

Customarily the statutes provide that prosecution is barred if a marriage between the parties takes place. It is this last feature of the statutes which has given seduction proceedings their ill repute. Surely, such statutes make all intercourse in contemplation of marriage a criminal offense in the male partner, though, as a legislative act of grace, prosecutions are barred or halted if the marriage does take place. The seduced girl wields a powerful weapon against her "seducer," should he prove to be a recalcitrant suitor. The result is likely to be a "seduction marriage," not unlike a "shotgun marriage," which is nonetheless usually regarded as valid. To prevent an abuse of this statute, whether the offense is alleged to rest on flattery, deceit or promise of marriage, or on any other ground, the statutes (or the courts) customarily impose the requirement of corroboration, and in many states the prosecutrix subjects her chastity to possible attack, for the purpose of discrediting the alleged marriage promise or stratagem, etc., on the defendant's part.

All states which have such a seduction statute—and not all do—have made this crime a felony. Prosecutions are not frequent, and those that are brought quite frequently smack of the justified spite of a pregnant girl or jilted bride.

Although the crime of abduction really belongs in a different category, because it does not require any intercourse, it is closely related to the felony of seduction. In many instances, indeed, abduction may merely amount to a preparatory offense for seduction. On the other hand, this offense is closely related to the crime of kidnapping. Insofar as I can generalize about the many abduction statutes in the various states, abduction is the taking of a female person, by either a male or a female person, and this taking must be by any one of various possible methods, like force, fraud, or even persuasion, for a certain purpose, like marriage, concubinage, sexual intercourse, prostitution, etc. The female victim is frequently required to be under a stated age. Most importantly, the taking must be *from* a specified person, like the parent, guardian, etc. Naturally, this raises the question as to who really is meant to be the protected person. As a matter of fact, some courts have flatly said that the parents are the victims of the offense—so that the consent of the minor girl, however it was obtained—is immaterial. More frequently, however, the statute is regarded as existing for the benefit of the female victim.

In our table we have also listed under abduction the offense of forced marriage, an extremely rare offense, and other offenses of a nature closely related to abduction. The cited statutes themselves must be consulted for details.

Abduction is a serious crime, a felony, though it is noteworthy that many states provide fines as an alternative to imprisonment, principally to provide for appropriate punishment in cases meeting the letter but not the spirit of the abduction laws. Such cases are not hard to imagine, especially in the case of divorced parents with divided custody rights, who disagree on the minor's prospective spouse.

39

Chapter 5
HOMOSEXUAL CONDUCT

Any discussion of homosexuality has to begin with a discussion of sodomy (or, occasionally buggery). The American colonies did not all have a law dealing specifically with sexual offenses. Virginia, for example, relied on the English "buggery" statute of 1533. Usually referred to as 25 Henry 8, Chapter 6, this statute made the "detestable and abominable Vice of Buggery," defined as homosexuality between two men or bestiality by men or women, a capital offense. The law may have stemmed from Henry VII's attack upon the church. For the first time in English history, homosexuality and bestiality, previously punishable in ecclesiastical courts as sins against God, now were punishable exclusively in civil courts as crimes against the state.

Nearly one hundred years after the statute became law, the great English jurist, Sir Edward Coke, expounding on all English laws in his *Institutes,* gave semi-official sanction to attitudes and beliefs about homosexuality that would influence justices of the peace on both sides of the Atlantic for the next two hundred years. In the Third Part of the *Institutes,* completed in 1628, Coke reinvoked religious sanction for the crime by stating that it was "against the ordinance of the Creator and order of nature." He also clarified the method of execution (hanging as opposed to burning or burying alive) and specified that some evidence of penetration was necessary for the crime. Buggery under English law, therefore, definitely meant anal intercourse by two men. Finally Coke wrote that if the party "buggered" were "within the age of discretion" (presumably meaning boys under fourteen years of age), he would not be guilty of the crime.

After the Revolution, Virginia pased its own buggery statute in 1792: " . . . if any do commit the detestable and abominable vice of Buggery, with man or beast, he or she so offending, shall be adjudged a felon and shall suffer death, as in case of felony, without benefit of Clergy." Ignorant of modern biological possibilities, 17th and 18th century Englishmen and Americans feared beastiality even more than homosexuality because they believed that inhuman creatures could be produced.

By 1800 the Virginia General Assembly repealed the death penalty for buggery, but only for free men. The crime now carried penalties from one to ten years in prison. The removal of the death penalty did not necessarily reflect any less opposition to the crime of buggery. In two hundred years of Virginia's history, there had been only one recorded execution for buggery. Despite the nearly complete absence of prosecutions, Virginia authorities still felt it necessary to keep the crime on the books, and even the reduced penalty was rather harsh when compared with other (heterosexual) offenses.

Virginia's experience and history with this offense was pretty much the American attitude toward homosexuality to the present. So great was (and perhaps still is) the fear, that Americans criminalized homosexuality from the very outset.

While there is no definitive statement as to what homosexuality is, we will offer here this fairly simple and generally accepted one: It is an erotic act consciously engaged in between two persons of the same sex. Homosexuality between consenting adults is a classic example of a crime without a victim, meaning that no one is hurt by the act unless it be the willing participants, that there is no complaint, and that it involves nothing more than an affront to the mores (and in the opinion of some people the mental health) of other members of society.

Illinois was the first state to repeal its laws against this type of behavior and even against street solicitation for "immoral purposes" but did not legalize prostitution. Several states followed Illinois in the decriminalization process, but most states continue to have laws against homosexual relations between adults both in public and in private. According to these penal codes, one may be subject to a lengthy term in prisom for violation of such laws, but there are few arrests and fewer long sentences and actual confinement. Those arrests that do occur are usually for activity in public or semipublic places.

Arrests for violation of the law with respect to homosexuality acts between consenting adults almost always involve either open solicitation of another person on the street or in some public place for the purpose of going to a private place to commit the act or apprehension during the commission of a

41

homosexual act in a public place, such as a washroom, a park, or an automobile.

In 1976, the United States Supreme Court upheld the constititionality of state anti-homosexual laws. The Court did not pass on the wisdom or propriety of such legislation but only on the right of the states to regulate the private consensual activity of adults; it found that the laws did not contravene any guarantee of freedom under the Bill of Rights of the Constitution. This meant, in effect, that further efforts to decriminalize adult consensual homosexual acts would have to be made in state legislatures (unless the Supreme Court were to review the matter in a different case and reverse itself).

Many of the anti-homosexual laws are vague, and they use phrases like "crimes against nature," which themselves are not spelled out. Early in the history of such legislation, the vagueness was deliberate for its was considered that these acts were "unmentionable" and "unspeakable," and hence could be written about only in the most circumspect manner lest the law itself become lewd and salacious. The laws are found under a variety of headings including "lewd and lascivious conduct," "indecent behavior," "buggery," "sodomy," and "unnatural sexual acts." Some of the penal codes define the terms and others do not; some have definitions contained in annotations from decisions or commentaries by judges of state appelate courts.

By and large, laws of this type have been marked by little or no enforcement effort or public demand for arrest and prosecution. Even those who are opposed to their repeal on the ground that the law should be the expression of the moral sentiment of the community do not favor investigation and prosecution of all cases where there is "probable cause" to believe that a crime has been committed.

As was indicated earlier, most arrests for homosexual activities take place because of the apprehension of the participants in an adult consensual act in a public or semi-public place like a restroom or a parked car, an alleyway or some similar place. In most cases, they are strangers to each other.

The American Law Institute proposes that the following be part of a penal code:

Section 251.3. Loitering to Solicit Deviate Sexual

42

> Relations. A person is guilty of a petty misdemeanor
> if he loiters in or near any public place for the purpose
> of solicity or being solicited to engage in deviate sex-
> ual relations.

Another paragraph, very general in its wording and hence likely to be attacked as unconstitutional if it were enacted into law, might also apply to homosexual cases:

> Section 251.1 Open Lewdness. A person commits
> a petty misdemeanor if he does any lewd act which
> he knows is likely to be observed by others who
> would be affronted or alarmed.

Together with homosexual conduct, the law considers sodomy and "crimes against nature" as serious perversions. Yet much of the sexual activity of husbands and wives also falls under the ban of sodomy and crime-against-nature statutes. Statutes like those of Minnesota, New York, and Washington, are quite specific about what "aberrant" sexual acts are pro-hibited:

1. carnal knowledge by or with the mouth of man by man
2. carnal knowledge by or with the mouth of man by woman
3. carnal knowledge by or with the mouth of woman by woman
5. carnal knowledge by the anus of man by man
6. carnal knowledge by the anus of woman by man
7. carnal knowledge of any animal or bird by man
8. carnal knowledge by any animal or bird by woman
9. sexual intercourse with a dead body

This last category of sexual aberration, known as necro-philia, is a medical curiosity.

But the point that becomes clear in the above catalog of prohibited acts is that the law proscribes sexual gratification by any other means than a "normal" act of sexual intercourse. Even masturbation may fall under the ban of sodomy and crimes against nature. For example, a Michigan statute subjects to five years imprisonment men who in public or private commit or are party to the commission of acts of gross indecency. This would presumable include mutual masturba-tion.

The penalties for indulging in sodomy and crimes against nature vary widely. They are, however, usually severe, sug-gesting that many legislatures have not shaken off the influence of the biblical injunction that death should be the lot of the sodomite, the homosexual, and persons committing bestiality. The penalties range from a one-year maximum in New York for a crime against nature with the consent of a person over eighteen years of age, to life imprisonment in Georgia or Nevada.

In short, sodomy and crimes against nature take place among heterosexual as well as homosexual parties. But the fact of the matter is that only a fractional portion of the homosexual and heterosexual activity that violates sodomy and crimes against nature statutes ever comes to the attention of law enforcement authorities. When the number of arrests and convictions are compared with the types of social situations which produce sodomistic acts and crimes against nature, with the estimates of homosexuality, and with reports on the incidence of unconventional methods of sexual satisfaction, it is clear that legal prohibitions against sodomy, homosexuality, and crimes against nature are practically unenforceable.

Sodomistic acts or crimes against nature normally come to the attention of the police department when children or minors are involved and parents complain, or where sexual activity is carried on so openly or with so little discretion that the police must take action. Both homosexuals and heterosexuals who observe reasonable discretion in their sexual activities and who leave minors alone have small fear from the police or prosecuting authorities.

Chapter 6
PROSTITUTION

Within the sphere of sexual offenses, no problem is harder to tackle, legally, sociologically or psychologically, than that of prostitution. This clearly is not the place to review the age-old failure of the law to repress this primeval commercial vice. Suffice it to say that the law has no intention to give up trying to repress prostitution by the methods at its command. Evidence gathered by the United Nations on a world-wide basis makes this course appear preferable to a permissive attitude of legalized and state-regulated prostitution.

The Prostitute

Within the broad sphere of prostitution we must distinguish between a wide variety of activities centering around the nucleus of the prostitute's activity. Following the order adopted for our tables, we shall first consider the act of the prostitute. Strictly speaking, it is not the act of prostitution which is punishable by these statutes, but rather, it is the status of being a prostitute, which is punishable, so that a further act of prostitution is simply the occasion which the law utilizes for prosecution. This is one of the few instances in which the criminal law imposes punishment not for conduct, but rather for status. (Vagrancy would be another example.)

Obviously, the status of being a prostitute is the result of conduct, namely promiscuous sexual intercourse with

45

more than one man. Theoretically, under many definitions, the payment of money to the woman for her services is not an element of the definition, though it may be. Unless the prosecution shows that the female defendant did have promiscuous intercourse with more than one man, the charge is not made out. On the other hand, theoretically, every female person who has engaged in promiscuous intercourse with more than one man, is a prostitute. Somehow, however, time heals all wounds, and it is altogether possible that a former prostitute may become a woman of chaste character. Any such adjudication depends very much on all the facts and circumstances and it is this which renders the crime an oddity. Generally, the punishment of prostitution is among the lowest for statutory offenses, and rehabilitation measures are often provided in the alternative or in addition, though with a relatively low degree of success.

The House of Prostitution

The keeping of houses of prostitution (bawdy houses, houses of ill fame, houses of assignation) was a misdemeanor at common law, in the nature of a nuisance, that is, a continuing activity of an annoying or an offensive character. Neither an isolated act of lewdness, nor even of lascivious intercourse, nor simply a bad reputation, render a house one of "ill fame." The house must be a common resort for the practice of prostitution, whether the prostitutes live there permanently or not, whether the activity is noisy or not, whether it reveals its character publicly or not.

Unlawful is the keeping, letting, renting, managing or owning of such houses, depending on the statutory wording. Several statutes punish residents, employees or agents as well. But only rarely does the punishment extend to the male person who frequents such a place, though conceivably he can be charged as a "disorderly person." Note the special statutory provisions on abatement of the nuisance in addition to punishment, revocation of liquor licenses, increased penalties if such houses are kept near particularly designated places, like schools, churches and fairgrounds.

Procurement

Having discussed the prostitute herself, and the house in which she practices her vocation, as well as the criminal liability of those connected with the house, I shall now turn to those (usually) male persons who facilitate the continuation of this criminal activity.

Pandering or procuring is the act of procuring a female person for a house of prostitution, with or without her consent, by means of promises, persuasion, trick, artifice or stratagem, threat or force, or similar means.

Most statutes subject to equal punishment any (male) person who in an equal manner retains or detains a prostitute in a house of ill fame for the purpose of prostitution. The statutes vary widely in the sweep of their coverage, and there is a frequent overlap of procuring prostitutes and employing them in houses of prostitution. Many such statutes also cover the transporting of female persons for purposes of prostitution. We have also included in this category the federal law prohibiting the transportation in interstate commerce of a female person for the purpose of prostitution, debauchery or any other immoral purpose. This law, although we have mentioned it specifically under the District of Columbia, governs equally any interstate transportation within the United States, or even into, or out of, the United States.

The punishments for these various activities vary widely, but the maximum punishments, applicable particularly to recidivists or aggravated cases, are quite high.

There is a frequent overlap with the general offense of abduction, and the offenses of pandering, procuring, etc. Thus offense requires no further discussion, except to comment that its principal purpose is the suppression of strong-arm and similar methods — for example, forceful detention for alleged debt, commonly used to recruit and maintain the army of prostitutes. Consequently, the penalties for this felony are severe.

Pimping

A pimp is definable as a male person who lives off the proceeds of a prostitute, or who takes money from the earnings of a prostitute or, sometimes, who merely resides with the prostitute. Occasionally a statute is phrased more directly in terms of his actual conduct in connection with prostitution, namely, the securing by him of a place in a bawdy house, for a prostitute. In sociological terms, the pimp is the prostitute's virtually indispensable bodyguard—as well as parasite. It is understandable that a law breaker subject to as much abuse as the prostitute, would seek the protection of a male person. Not infrequently this "protector" teams up with the prostitute for the purpose of committing such offenses as robbery, assault, larceny, blackmail or extortion, on unsuspecting customers.

In our last sub-category we turn to erring relatives of the prostitute, namely husbands who are subjected to special punishments for causing their wives to engage in prostitution—a statute existing in about one third of the states, and the parent who consents to or fosters the prostitution of a child. That such abominable activities should be deterred by threat of severe punishment, nobody will doubt, yet occasionally such is only a misdemeanor.

As previously indicated, city ordinances are not discussed in this book. On a topic like prostitution, however, the consideration of city ordinances is mandatory for those who have to deal with the problem.

PROPOSED REFORM

Prostitution is illegal in all states except Nevada where county autonomy is permitted. As a result, Nevada has legal houses of prostitution in several of its counties. But solicitation in public and semi-public places continues to be illegal. Other than this Nevada situation, there are many variations in the legal definitions of the act, the efforts at enforcement, the courtroom procedures, the allowable and actual sentences, and the types of law under which the prostitute, customer, pimp, madam, or some other associated person can be arrested.

Although patronizing a prostitute is illegal in many states, arrests on this charge are rare. New York State offers a very specific statute in this connection:

A person is guilty of patronizing a prostitute when:

1. *Pursuant to a prior understanding, he pays a fee to another person as compensation for such person or a third person having engaged in sexual conduct with him; or*

2. *He pays or agrees to pay a fee to another person to an understanding that in return therefor such a person or a third person will engage in sexual conduct with him; or*

3. *He solicits or requests another person to engage in such conduct with him in return for a fee.*

There are, however, many states in which patronizing a prostitute is not illegal. This probably reflects society's attitude toward prostitution, that is, it is not the act that is reviled but rather the woman who participates in it. Beyond this, there is limited public opinion and judicial support for prostitution arrests in an era when crime rates are high and deployment of police personnel for the arrest of muggers, rapists, and other serious criminals, is perceived as a more compelling need.

Arrests for prostitution do occur, but largely reflect the pressures on police than the extent of this activity.

The Model Penal Code of the American Law Institute has a section dealing with prostitution. This act is not grouped with sexual offenses (forcible sex, corruption of minors, indecent exposure) or with offenses against the family (polygamy, incest, abortion) but rather is part of a category called "public indecency" itself part of a larger class of crimes labeled "offenses against public order and decency." Public indecency consists of open lewdness, prostitution and related offenses, loitering to solicit deviant sexual relations, and obscenity. The proposals of the American Law Institute with regard to prostitution and related offenses read as follows:

Section 251.2 Prostitution and Related Offenses.

(1) Prostitution. *A person is guilty of prostitution, a petty misdemeanor, if he or she:*

    (a) is an inmate of a house of prostitution or otherwise engages in sexual activity as a business; or

    (b) loiters in or within view of any public place for the purposes of being hired to engage in sexual activity.

"Sexual activity" includes homosexual and other deviate sexual relations. A "house of prostitution" is any place where prostitution or promotion of prostitution is regularly carried on by one person under the control, management or supervision of another. An "inmate" is a person who engages in prostitution in or through the agency of a house of prostitution. "Public place" means any place to which the public or any substantial group thereof has access.

(2) Promoting Prostitution. A person who knowingly promotes prostitution of another commits a misdemeanor or felony as provided in Subsection (3). The following acts shall, without limitation of the foregoing, constitute promoting prostitution:

- *(a) owning, controlling, managing supervising, or otherwise keeping, alone or in association with others, a house of prostitution or a prostitution business; or*
- *(b) procuring an inmate for a house of prostitution or a place in a house of prostitution for one who would be an inmate; or*
- *(c) encouraging, inducing, or otherwise purposely causing another to become or remain a prostitute; or*
- *(d) soliciting a person to patronize a prostitute; or*
- *(e) procuring a prostitute for a patron; or*
- *(f) transporting a person into or within this state with purpose to promote that person's engaging in prostitution, or procuring or paying for transportation with that purpose; or*
- *(g) leasing or otherwise permitting a place controlled by the actor, alone or in association with others, to be regularly used for prostitution or the promotion of prostitution, or failure to make reasonable effort to abate such use by ejecting the tenant, notifying law enforcement authorities, or other legally available means; or*
- *(h) soliciting, receiving, or agreeing to receive any benefits for doing or agreeing to do anything forbidden by this Subsection.*

(3) Grading of Offenses Under Subsection *(2) An offense under Subsection (2) constitutes a felony of the third degree if:*

(a) the offense falls within paragraph (a), (b) or (c) of
Subsection (2); or

(b) the actor compels another to engage in or promote
prostitution; or

(c) the actor promotes prostitution of a child under 16,
whether or not he is aware of the child's age; or

(d) the actor promotes the prostitution of his wife, child,
ward or any person for whose care, protection or
support he is responsible. Otherwise the offense is a
misdemeanor.

(4) Presumption from Living off Prostitutes. *A person,
other than the prostitute or the prostitute's minor child or legal
dependent incapable of self-support, who is supported in whole
or in substantial part by the proceeds of prostitution is presumed to be knowingly promoting prostitution in violation of
Subsection (2).*

(5) Patronizing Prostitutes. *A person commits a violation if
he hires a prostitute to engage in sexual activity with him, or if
he enters or remains in a house of prostitution for the purpose
of engaging in sexual activity.*

(6) Evidence. *On the issue whether a place is a house of
prostitution the following shall be admissible evidence: its
general repute; the repute of the persons who reside in or
frequent the place; the frequency, timing and duration of visits
by non-residents. Testimony of a person against his spouse
shall be admissible to prove offenses under this Section.*

Efforts to decriminalize prostitution have met with little or
no success despite the efforts of civil libertarians. Some state
bar associations, however, have in fact adopted resolutions
calling for such decriminalization, but the American Bar
Association, has time and again narrowly defeated this kind of
resolution. Every jurisdiction in the country has laws
regulating prostitution, soliciting for prostitution or loitering
for the purpose of prostitution. Numerous court challenges
have been made attacking either the prostitution laws
themselves or the methods of police enforcement. So far the
existing laws and police procedures have survived most
attacks.

Chapter 7

SEXUAL OFFENSES AGAINST CHILDREN AND MINORS

CHILD MOLESTATION

This category of sexual offense and/or crime includes terms like "carnal abuse" of a child, "child abuse," "impairing the morals of a minor," and "statutory rape." Like other crimes, these are defined in a variety of ways in different penal codes and in the various states.

While "statutory rape" legally includes only sexual relations in which intercourse takes place or penetration is accomplished, "child molestation" and "impairing the morals of a minor" cover any sexual contact at all between an adult and a minor, from the touching of the buttocks of a child to completing a sexual act.

The offense of "impairing the morals of a child" or "of a minor" is usually a lesser offense than molestation and therefore offers plea bargaining possibilities. Furthermore, although the terms are most frequently used for matters relating to sex, they are applied to non-sexual matters as introducing a minor into crime by encouraging theft although this would be more likely to be prosecuted as "contributing to the delinquency of a minor." To impair the morals of a child in a sexual event, one need not have made overtures to, or have had contact with, the child; the impairment can be through teaching, encouraging, or making possible such sexual contact with others or even through permitting and encouraging the child to witness such events. Showing pornographic films or other such materials to a child, taking a minor to a brothel, gay bar or obscene exhibition, selling or giving contraceptives to a child below the age of sexual consent, are all subsumed under "impairing the morals of a minor."

The key question in the determination of an offense of a sexual nature under the rubric of child molestation involves the age of the child; as a secondary question, the age of the offender is also relevant. What adultchild sexuality concerns is essentially some form of sexual confrontation between a person over the age of eighteen and a child much younger than the age of consent and hence a more aggravated offense than statutory rape.

Concealment of age by the younger of the partners in a willing relationship is generally unacceptable as a defense in sex cases involving minors or teenagers, and never acceptable in cases in which one partner is a child, usually defined as under twelve years old. The American Law Institute has proposed compromise to the defense that the offender did not know that she (or he) "was that young." Its suggestion is that if the child is under ten no such defense is permissible, but between ten and the legal age of consent where it is substantiated by the general appearance of the minor and other relevant evidence, such a defense should be contemplated.

Subsection 213.2 Corruption of Minors and Seduction

(1) Offense Defined. *A male who has sexual intercourse with a female not his wife, or any person who engages in deviate sexual intercourse or causes another to engage in deviate sexual intercourse, is guilty of an offense if;*

> *(a) the other person is less than (   ) years old and the actor is at least (   ) years older than the other person.*

Subsection 213.6 Provisions Generally Applicable to Article 213.

(1) Mistake as to Age. *Whenever in this Article the criminality of conduct depends o a child's being below the age of 10, it is no defense that the actor did not know the child's age, or reasonably believed the child to be older than 10. When criminality depends on the child's being below a critical age other than 10, it is a defense for the actor to prove that he reasonably believed the child to be above the critical age.*

STATUTORY RAPE

In the case of intercourse with minors under a specified age limit, all legislatures have passed special "statutory rape" legislation, which makes such intercourse rape, although usually subject to a reduced punishment. Here, too, "force" is not required, and, in fact, *factually* there may be consent, but the law deems it immaterial, for the minor's protection. Nevertheless, if a minor is truly raped, i.e., by real force, and against her will, the perpetrator will be charged with true rape, rather than with statutory rape.

Many legislatures have recognized the fact that juveniles pass through an age of sexual curiosity and experimentation. Rightfully, the law considers these activities of teenagers with less reprobation than the act of a mature adult, committed on an immature adolescent or even child. In New York, for example, when the perpetrator is less than twenty-one years old (and the "victim" is below the age of eighteen years), the offense is merely a misdemeanor "rape," subject to a relatively mild punishment. But if the intercourse with a minor girl, below the age of eighteen, is committed by a defendant who is twenty-one years old or older, the offense is rape in the second degree, standing midway between misdemeanor rape and rape in the first degree (with actual force and without actual consent).

Recognizing the fact that the criminality of statutory rape seeks to protect the purity of young girls, a number of state statutes require that the victim actually be of previous chaste character, which is not necessarily identical with virginity. Clearly, unless there are other circumstances present, marriage with consequent surrender of virginity does not deprive the female person of her chaste character. Thus, a very young widow may well be the victim of statutory rape. If evidence to the contrary is adduced, the offense is not statutory rape. (In some states "previous chaste character" is merely an evidentiary matter to be taken into consideration in assessing the question of actual consent in outright rape cases.) Needless to say, if it was the defendant himself who terminated the victim's previous chaste character, he cannot avail himself of the defense.

In several sexual offenses, but especially in statutory rape, the misuse of a relation of trust or dependency (teacher-student relation, for example), is frequently an aggravating circumstance.

A word about absolute age limits is called for. In several states, the common law rule still prevails that a boy below the age of fourteen years is irrebuttably presumed to be incapable of engaging in sexual relations. Thus, he cannot be found guilty of offenses like rape or statutory rape. In other states this is a rebuttable presumption, which may be overcome by evidence to the contrary.

As to girls, several state statutes posit a minimum age for girls beyond which—quite apart from legal consent—no factual consent is regarded as possible, so that any intercourse with girls below that age would be actual rape, rather than statutory rape. Historically, the limit was placed at ten years, and statutes vary therefrom to some extent.

As an aside, cases have been reported in which the victim was as young as not even one year, or as old as eighty-six years.

The law supposes always that in cases of statutory rape the minor female is the victim and the boy the reprehensible aggressor. This may not always correspond to reality, but the law will not recognize it. But in several states it is now an offense for an adult woman to have intercourse with a minor male partner. This is statutory rape in reverse.

Like rape, statutory rape is commonly a felony, a grave offense, subject to severe punishment (though usually less than that provided for forceful rape), although as discussed, the *actual* guilt of the perpetrator may be but slight. Special sets of punishments usually exist when the age discrepancy between perpetrator and victim is either particularly small or particularly large.

Reliable statistics on the frequency of statutory rape are not available. The estimates of some scientists as to the number of female persons of high school age who have had premarital intercourse range as high as 50% for the United States. Most such acts of intercourse were in the nature of statutory rape. The percentage figure varies, incidentally, in accordance with such factors as educational attainment, intelligence, socio-economic background, etc.

Needless to say, there is absolutely no correlation between the estimated number of technical offenses and the number of prosecutions and convictions.

Incest

Incest, like rape and statutory rape, consists of heterosexual intercourse. But here the similarity ends, for incest is the sexual intercourse between relatives within the prohibited degrees of relationship. Unless one of the parties is incapable of incurring criminal liability (e.g., by reason of infancy), both persons involved in the incest are guilty, —equally guilty. Since the common law left the prosecution and punishment of incest to the law of the church (the ecclesiastical law), incest is a completely statutory crime in our states. Some states regard as incest also the mere marriage (ceremony) between closely related parties. Most statutes include within the sweep of incest all relationships nearer than first cousins, some include first cousins. Relationship by affinity (by marriage) is frequently included together with the more obvious relationship by consanguinity (blood relationship).

Incest, traditionally, has been regarded as one of the most serious offenses, and popular thought continues that tradition, while professionals, looking at offenders with more skeptical eyes, frequently find persons engaging in incestual relationships to be of deviant or abnormal psychic make-up.

Incest is universally a felony, subject to a penitentiary sentence, though the terms vary from state to state. Statistics on incest are not available, but its occurrence is extremely low.

Chapter 8
SEXUAL PRIVACY LEGISLATION

Laws regulating sexual behavior today, or at least most of these laws, had been enacted in the late 19th century and the earliest years of the 20th century. These codes undoubtedly reflected society's attitudes of that period. Equally as undoubtedly, these attitudes have changed radically as we come within shouting distance of the 21st century.

In the late 1950's, the American Law Institute, with the assistance of judges, lawyers, and legal scholars, drafted a "Model Penal Code" as a guide for the various state legislatures that were about to launch a wholesale revision of their penal codes. One of the most controversial recommendations of the A.L.I. was the decriminalization of private sex acts between consenting adults. In 1960, Illinois became the first state to adopt this A.L.I. recommendation. The age of sexual consent was set at eighteen years. In addition, Illinois decriminalized noncommercial sexual solicitations between adults.

Since the decriminalization in Illinois, an additional twenty-two legislatures have voted to decriminalize private sexual acts between consenting adults:

Alaska	Nebraska
Arkansas	New Hampshire
California	New Jersey
Colorado	New Mexico
Connecticut	North Dakota
Delaware	Ohio
Hawaii	Oregon
Idaho	South Dakota
Indiana	Washington
Iowa	West Virginia
Maine	

In Idaho, decriminalization never took effect because the legislature repealed the sexual provision before the effective date of the new code. In Arkansas, sexual reform was operative for one year, and then its legislature re-enacted provisions for private homosexual behavior, retaining decriminalization for heterosexuals.

These legislative changes do not necessarily reflect important changes in popular attitudes or mores. The strategies by which these changes have occurred suggest otherwise. In only one of these states was a bill specifically designed to decriminalize private sex for adults. In two states decriminalization was accomplished through reform of rape laws. In the remaining states decriminalization was hidden in the general penal code reform package. Usually the chances for passage of sexual-law reform are greatly enhanced when it is part of a bill containing hundreds of other statutory changes. The chances of the public, the church, or conservative legislatures opposing the bill are thereby greatly minimized.

California is the only state in the country that has de-criminalized by ways of a special bill. In 1975 the vote in the state senate was a tie. When conservative senators threatened to leave the senate floor to break the quorum, they were locked in the room for several hours until the lieutenant governor was flown back to Sacramento from Denver to cast the deciding vote in favor of decriminalization.

In the mid-1960's the New York legislature passed a general penal code revision. The proposed decriminalization of private sex was strongly opposed by the Catholic Church. As a result, the legislature compromised and decriminalized for married couples only. Acts of oral copulation or sodomy between consenting single persons remain criminal acts in New York.

The Texas legislature reformed its sex laws when it revised its entire penal code in the early 1970's. It decriminalized for all consenting heterosexuals but retained homosexual conduct as an infraction.

Ever since its landmark decision in 1965, *Griswold v. Connecticut,* the United States Supreme Court has been developing the constitutional right of sexual privacy. In this landmark decision the Court voided a law that infringed on the rights of married couples to use contraceptives. The Court acknowledged that a right of marital privacy existed and told the government to get out and stay out of the marital bedroom.

A few years later the Court expanded this "marital right of privacy" in the case of *Eisenstadt v. Baird*. Here the Court said that single persons also have a right to privacy and that the state could not forbid their use of contraceptives. In the early 1970's the Court again expanded the right of privacy to a series of abortion cases beginning with *Roe v. Wade*. The right of privacy was held to be so fundamental that the state could not prohibit abortions during the first trimester.

Civil libertarians are looking for the time when this sexual right of privacy might actually be extended by the Court to include the right to engage in private sexual behavior by consenting adults without interference by statutory prohibitions and regulations. Relying on the *Griswold, Eisenstadt,* and *Roe* cases, several appellate courts and federal courts have indicated that statutes prohibiting such private behavior are unconstitutional. Proponents of decriminalization seemed to be gaining momentum in the courts under *Doe v. Commonwealth's Attorney*. Two anonymous homosexuals filed suit in federal district court in Virginia attacking that state's sodomy law. Virginia law forbids engaging in oral or anal sex, whether married, single, heterosexual, or homosexual. The federal court, in a two-to-one decision, upheld the state law. The anonymous homosexuals appealed to the United States Supreme Court. That Court upheld the lower federal court's decision without granting a hearing or permitting oral arguments.

In the areas of contraception and abortion, the nation's highest Court has extended the right of privacy to juveniles. In *Planned Parenthood of Central Missouri v. Danforth*, the Court declared as unconstitutional laws that required parental consent to an abortion for a minor. In another case in 1977, *Carey v. Population Services International*, the Court declared as unconstitutional laws that made it a crime to distribute contraceptives to minors under sixteen. Arguments were made that this prohibition was necessary in order to discourage premarital sex among teenagers. The Court held that it would not allow this type of approach to curb teenage promiscuity. Noting that it had not yet definitively decided to what extent states may regulate private sexual behavior among adults, it declined to decide which constitutional rights minors may have regarding sexual behavior.

Although legislative and judicial development of sexual privacy has been somewhat slow-paced, proponents gained considerable leverage when, in 1973, the American Bar Association adopted a resolution urging all state legislatures to decriminalize sexual activity among consenting adults.

Chapter 9

PORNOGRAPHY AND OBSCENITY

Statutes broadly grouped in this category—some of which actually bear this title—cover a wide variety of forbidden sexual activities short of intercourse. Among them are masturbation, molestation of others, especially children, any sexually motivated or genitally directed touching or fondling without consent or as a public annoyance, any accosting or soliciting for such a purpose, assaults and batteries of indecent or immoral nature, and so on. It is absolutely impossible to describe the enormous variety which exists among fifty-two jurisdictions as to what the statutes of this nature cover. In addition, one should constantly bear in mind that what in one state is covered by a statute on indecent liberties may well be touched upon elsewhere under a broadly phrased sodomy statute, or may have been separately regulated by specific statutes on voyerism or exhibitionism, and so on.

It is under this heading that in practice we frequently meet with the pedophiliac, the aged man who, with various degrees of an age-conditioned deterioration of his psychic and emotional processes, seeks contact with young children, male or female. The contact he seeks is not necessarily superdetermined by sexual desires. It may be but the pursuit of a substitute for the show of fondness he once had in family relations that no longer exist. Yet the public hysteria of the stalking monster who molests and slays little children frequently lands such lonely old men in jail for little more than a fond pat bestowed on the imaginative little daughter of hypersensitive or hysterical parents.

On the other hand, the pedophiliac may well seek and practice sexual contact with children who are bound to suffer from the emotional shock which such an experience entails. Just as we must concede to the state the power and duty to remove garbage—which cannot help being garbage—from the street, we must grant it the right to remove noxious and harmful adults,—who *often* cannot help being such—from the streets. But we should insist that their noxiousness and harmful tendency be clearly established. Even then, however, the penal law cannot put much trust in its deterrent effect. Particularly in this sphere of the biologically deviant sexual offender, we must employ the aid of medical science and the social services.

Voyerism and Exhibitionism

What has been said about the pedophiliac goes in large measure for the voyerist and exhibitionist.

Just as any mature or aged adult has a natural desire to convey fondness to children—which has deep-rooted and usually unknown sexual origins—so every human being has a natural desire to see sexually stimulating views, or to show off in a sexually stimulating manner. The law is cognizant of such natural psychological phenomena and makes no attempt to suppress them all. What it does attempt to suppress is the abnormal excess of desire in all these respects and, of course, what is normal depends very much on time, place and circumstance.

VOYERISM Persons with slight psychic or emotional disturbances who are abnormal in their desire to "see" are called voyerists or, more popularly, Peeping Toms. Their activities in transgression of the public limits of the normal (the normal being the viewing of fashionably dressed persons or of theatrical performances and the like) are punishable by law, usually as a misdemeanor subject to minor punishments, and frequently only under loitering statutes and city ordinances, though in several states under specific state statutes. Their abnormalities generally are not such that the law can absolve them from all liability. The threat of punishment is tailored in such a way as to curb *their* excessive curiosity and propensity, for persons without the propensity need no such additional penal stimulus. If they transgress nevertheless, the law must execute the threat. The mere experience on their part that the law *means* what it says, however, is often not sufficient to render them capable of living up to the legal standard in the future. Hence, confinement must be accompanied by social or psychiatric treatment efforts, and such is frequently not forthcoming.

EXHIBITIONISM   The exhibitionist is a basically not dissimilar offender. In our tables we have made an effort to distinguish between non-commercial exhibitionism, which generally tends in the direction of the psycho-pathological, and commercial or theatrical exhibitionism, which is discussed below.

Exhibitionism in the stricter sense ranges all the way from the psycho-pathological act of indecent exposure of the genitalia in front of surprised and shocked passers-by (strangers), almost always committed by men, to the relatively harmless act of wearing a somewhat risqué Bikini bathing suit in a conservative resort town. Occasionally even a harmless man, woman or child, may get trapped in the nets of this law, in the act of relieving himself at a more or less public spot where he believes himself unobserved, but is not.

In addition to the state statutes which prohibit such offensive conduct, there are many local ordinances in point, and the standards have wide variations as to what is considered suitable coverage of the private parts of the human body and what is "indecent exposure." But the typical, psycho-pathological exhibitionist who commits his act for personal sexual excitement or satisfaction obviously is covered by all such statutes. These offenders customarily do not intend to rape or assault their baffled victims, so that charges of attempted rape are not called for. Obviously, psychiatric treatment is indicated for such offenders, but they are, generally, found responsible for their conduct, whenever they are capable of some control of their actions. The punishments are mild, and usually do not range beyond one year of detention in a jail.

These statutes also frequently cover the practice of nudism, which is a socialized form of exhibitionism, i.e., one which lacks the erotic appeal among those who join in the practice. Since organized nudism is practiced on private property and concealed from public view, there is no reason for the law to intervene, because such exposures simply are not "indecent." In an appeal from a judgment of conviction for indecent exposure, the Michigan Supreme Court properly found that the only indecency that was committed was that of the raiding police officers: "It was indecent— indeed the one big indecency we find in this whole case: descending upon those unsuspecting souls like storm troopers; herding them before clicking cameras like plucked chickens; hauling them away in police cars. . . ."

The law, we teach our students in law school, is a jealous mistress. Occasionally, as in the case of nudism, it is a rather meddlesome mistress.

The offenses discussed in this chapter are abnormal sexual behaviors in our society, practiced by individuals of clearly aberrant mentality. Prison alone serves no purpose for such offenders because penal institutions do not remove the mental conflicts which cause the indecencies in the first place. The result is repeated acts. Strong therapy is probably the important requirement in these matters. Punishment serves neither the defendant nor future offended parties.

Commercial Obscenity

Until very recently obscenity was one of the most uncertain topics among sexual or, rather, sex-related, offenses. To be quite sure, this is still a confusing topic, but due to recent Supreme Court litigation, the topic has become much clearer, as to definition, constitutional protection and censorial regulation.

First of all, the concept of obscenity has been clarified. A publication is obscene or indecent if, "to the average person, applying contemporary community standards, the dominant theme of the material taken as a whole appeals to prurient interests." In thus supplying a definition of obscenity, the Supreme Court indicated that broadly phrased statutes will be regarded as constitutional. This new standard still is a rather general one, but this is meant to be its strength, since what gives it meaning is the prevailing standard of the community in which the alleged obscenity is charged to have been published. Laymen on the jury are supposedly able to apply such a standard—provided they are told what "prurient" means. (Prurient has nothing to do with the Puritans, it means itching, longing, especially lasciviously longing.) This standard is calculated to reach "dirt for dirt's sake," "filth for filth's sake." State interpretations of the word "obscene" still may differ from this federal standard, but it has been gaining ground ever since first proposed in the Model Penal Code of the American Law Institute.

Second, the Supreme Court has unmistakably ruled that the constitutional protection of freedom of speech and of the press (First Amendment to the United States Constitution) does not extend to obscene matter; and thirdly, at least as far as motion pictures are concerned, a pre-publication restraint through municipal censorship has been held permissible—very much to the surprise of constitutional law experts and all civil liberties-minded citizens. This last move is the more surprising since there was no indication that the criminal law, with its threat of punishment for publication of obscene matter, could not properly regulate the situation. While the Supreme Court emphatically limited its decision to the permissibility of (local) motion picture censorship, it has long committed itself to treating motion pictures and other mass communications media alike, so that there is justified fear that some day in the future local morals censorship of other mass communications media likewise will be held permissible. For the time being, however, law enforcement is entitled to intervene only *after* the fact of publication has occurred, as to all non-motion picture publications.

If we are agreed upon the potential danger which the mass publication of indecent and obscene material has—and, as indicated earlier, there is by no means unanimity on that question—punishment as a preventive must be carefully considered. The commercial offender, more than any other, takes calculated risks. He will weigh the likelihood of prosecution and the severity of a possible punishment before deciding to publish. When he does publish, the price of his publication is likely to be large enough to absorb any possible fine and still leave a handsome profit. Fines are therefore a poor deterrent for the commercial offender, and imprisonment is by far preferable. Our statutes provide for both, but the maximum sentences of imprisonment are ordinarily not large enough to deter, and fines are much too frequently imposed.

MASS PUBLICATION OF OBSCENITY (Table 1A)

What is punishable under these mass publication statutes is the production, offering for sale, sale, distribution, etc., of obscene materials, of the nature covered by the statutes (books, magazines, periodicals, pictures, films, records, etc.) Special provision is usually made for the more severe punishment of defendants who have made such material available to children.

Obscene advertising is usually covered by special provisions. Although not exclusively, such statutes are ordinarily directed against the advertising of contraceptives or other merchandise or services in some way connected with the reproductive organs.

Likewise punishable by many statutes in any theatrical obscenity, i.e., state, nightclub, or cabaret performance, whether through indecent exposure of the person, word of mouth, or any other thespian method.

Non-Commercial Obscenity

Long before our law found it necessary to deal specifically with the obscenity of mass communications media, there existed laws punishing any public indecency. The harm which the mass media are likely to create if they publish obscenities is one directed at the very moral standard of a whole citizenry, one of long range potential, while the harm of an undisseminated obscenity, hurled from one person to another, is of a short range potential. It is, thus, an indignity inflicted only on the immediate surroundings. Nevertheless, even here many statutes insist, and many decisions hold, that the obscenity must be such as to disturb the public peace. This would, ordinarily, exempt an obscene insult, directed by one person against another in private, or by letter or telephone. To protect the citizen even against private insults of an obscene nature, many statutes specifically cover such situations. Thus, our tables are classified so as to mention specifically all obscenities, whether by word of mouth, writing, letter, telephone, picture or gesture, under special consideration of those statutes which cover obscenities at particular locations. The divisions are self-explanatory.

GLOSSARY OF COMMON AND UNCOMMON SEXUAL WORDS AND PHRASES

Accost term used by police and prosecutors to describe approaches in public, by males or females, for sexual solicitation.

Age of consent statutory age, differing from state to state, which defines the legal capacity of a minor to give informed consent to sexual relations; to have sexual relations, even with consent, with a minor below the age of consent constitutes a crime (see statutory rape)

Buggery anal sodomy

Bull dyke masculine lesbian

Butch masculine lesbian

Call boy male prostitute available for home or hotel visits through a central telephone answering service or registry

Call girl female prostitute available for hotel or home visits through a telephone answering service or registry; usually higher priced and more attractive than street walkers or brothel prostitutes

Carnal knowledge of a minor charge brought against an adult who has had copulative or sodomistic relations, no matter how slight the penetration, with a minor

Castration a sexualization; surgical excision of the male testes

Cat house house of prostitution

Catamite homosexual prostitute or kept boy

Celibacy state of sustained virginity; refraining from sexual relations and/or marriage, often for religious reasons

Chancroid visible symptom of venereal infection

Cherry the hymen; a virgin

Chicken young male, usually in early adolescence, who makes himself available for sexual acts with older male partners, generally for money

Child molester person, usually male, who seeks sexual satisfaction from very young children

Circumcision surgical removal of foreskin of penis for religious or hygienic reasons

Clap gonorrhea

Clitoridectomy surgical removal of all or part of clitoris

Cohabit formerly used as euphemism for regular or at least repeated copulation between a male and female not married to each other; later tended to be restricted to such couples when domiciling together

Cohabitation, lewd and lascivious charge brought in some states against those living together openly without marriage to each other

Coitus interruptus withdrawal of the penis from the vagina before emission to prevent unwanted pregnancy

Community standards phrase used by the U.S. Supreme Court which would define material as pornographic and subject to criminal sanction if patently offensive in a given area

Condom contraceptive device placed over penis to prevent entry of semen into woman's body; also used for prevention of venereal disease (prophylactic); rubber

Consensual acts generic term covering acts between two or more persons that take place by mutual consent, with no threat or use of force; usually restricted to acts between adults

Consummate the process of completing the marital union by having sexual intercourse

Continence refraining from sexual relations by act of will

Contraceptive a device, medication, or method used to prevent pregnancy

Contributing to the delinquency of a minor charge brought against an adult who exposes a child to a situation that might result in delinquent acts, i.e., introducing a child to narcotics, suggesting that a child commit a crime, encouraging homosexual activity or act with prostitute

Coprolalia, coprophasia, coprophilia sexual stimulation and/or satisfaction from use of or listening to obscene language or stories, especially those focusing on excrement

Copulatio analis anal sodomy

Cornelia complex incestuous desire of mother for her son

Cross-dressing transvestism

Cunnilinguis oral contact with the female labia

Degenerate police-prosecutorial term for a person engaging in almost any form of disvalued or criminalized sexual activity

Demi-vierge literally a "half-virgin," used to denote a female who engages in many types of sexual activity except copulation; technical virgin

Detumescence the proces of going from the erect to the flaccid state of the penis, normally occurring following ejaculation

Deviate, sexual one whose sexual drive or focus is directed toward socially unaccepted channels; most often used for child molester

Dildo artificial penis

Drag queen effeminate homosexual who wears female clothing, jewelry, and may impersonate female

Dyke lesbian

Ejaculation emission of seminal fluid. (emission either prior to penetration or prior to readiness of female partner; ejaculatio praecox)

Premature ejaculation emission prior to penetration or prior to readiness of female partner; ejaculatio praecox

Electra complex excessive, perhaps incestuous, interest in daughter in her father, including unconscious interest

Emasculate asexualize, castrate; used literally and figuratively

Entrapment vice squad technique in which either a plain-clothesman or a decoy working with him inveigles homosexual or prostitute into soliciting, for the purpose of making arrest; widely used in criminal jurisprudence for nonsexual matters

Eonism transvestism, cross-dressing, drag

Erection the state of sexually stimulated, tumescent penis; term is sometimes used when there is stimulation and hardening of clitoris or nipples

Erogenous zones areas of body particularly sensitive to sexual stimulation

Erotographomania conduct in which major sexual satisfaction is derived from viewing sexually explicit paintings, sculpture, or other objects

Erotolalia deriving major sexual satisfaction from talking about or listening to talk about sex

Erotomania compulsive interest in sexual matters

Erotophilic strong interest in and concentration on erotic matters

Erotophobic afraid of sex, hostile to evidences of sexuality

Estrogen female sex hormone

Estrus in heat, ready for sex

Eunich an emasculated male, asexualized, castrated

Exhibitionist one deriving sexual satisfaction from the showing of one's genitals to unwilling viewers

Extracoital sexual connection between male and female not involving penetration of the vagina; may be oral, anal, inter-mammary, interfemoral, or other

Fag, faggot pejorative term used either for an effeminate homosexual or for a homosexual regardless of outward manifestations of effeminacy

Fellatio, fellation taking the penis into the mouth; the recipient can be male, or female

Fellator male insertee in fellatio

Fellatrix female insertee in fellatio

Fetishism the focus of the sex drive on a part of the body rather than on the person (usually not on the genitals), or on some bodily function, or on some inanimate object, often clothing, odorous object, etc.

Fetishist one who has strong fetishistic compulsions

Flagellation a form of sadomasochism in which sexual satisfaction is obtained from whipping or being whipped

Foreplay stimulation by touching, licking, tickling, pinching, kissing, or in some other form, prior to copulation, and not as an end in itself

Fornication copulation between a male and female neither of whom is married

Frigidity inability to respond to sexual stimulation

Frotteur a person who frequents crowded places for the purpose of rubbing against the bodies of others

Gay homosexual

Gay liberation movement to secure rights for homosexuals, to destigmatize behavior, decriminalize homosexuality, and end discrimination

Gerontosexuality abnormal desire of a younger person for sexual relations with a much older male or female

Gonorrhea venereal disease characterized by an emission from the penis; clap

Granuloma inquinale serious venereal disease

Hermaphroditism possession of some male and some female sex organs by one person; ambiguity as to whether the individual is male or female

Heterosexual pertaining to individual or sex drive oriented toward gratification with other sex

Homoerotophobia fear of being or being considered homosexual, also fear of homosexuality

Homophile homosexual, and particularly associated with gay liberation movements; literally, love of same

Homosexuality pertaining to individual or sex drive oriented toward gratification with same sex

Homosexual marriage long-term monogamous homosexual relationships, not recognized as legal marriages, but consecrated as marital union by a few homosexually oriented churches

Hooker a prostitute

Horny sexually stimulated; if male, perhaps tumescent

Hustler a male or female prostitute; also used for nonsexual connotations, as drug hustler

Hymen the membrane which closes the opening to the vagina in virgins; cherry

Impairing the morals of a minor charge brought against adults, lesser than carnal abuse, often but not always for sex-related offense, as fondling a child's genitals, showing child pornographic material, or photographing a child engaged in sex play with other children

Impotence a condition in which the male is physiologically or psychologically unable to get or maintain an erection at the time of intercourse; occasionally used to decribe the female

Incest sexual relations between persons of close blood kinship relationship; legally usally extended to relationships by adoption or through marriage other than between spouses

Indecent exposure exhibitionism; exposure of the genitals in public even if no sexual motivation is present, as in public urination, nude swimming, or sunbathing

Infantosexuality focus of sexual desire on very young (pre-pubertal) children

Intercourse term usually restricted to penile-vagina copulation

Interfemoral coitus placing the tumescent penis between the tightly closed thighs of partner and reaching emission through friction; thighing

Intermammary coitus placing the tumescent penis between the breasts of partner and effecting emission by friction

Intersexuality hermaphroditism; possessing some of the physical and/or psychological characteristics of both genders

Intrauterine device contraceptive which prevents sperm from entering the womb; IUD

John customer of prostitute, usually used for heterosexual prostitution; trick is synonym used for homosexual and heterosexual customer

Kept boy, kept girl male (or female) supported, usually by older man, in return for sex favors

Leather bar gathering place, particularly bar, for homosexual sadomasochists, rough trade, motorcycle crowd, and apparently virile type of homosexuals

Lesbianism female homosexuality, sapphism, tribalism

Lewd and lascivious police-prosecutorial term to describe criminalized, depraved, disvalued and perverse sexual behaviors

Libido sexual drive

Masochism deriving sexual satisfaction from having pain inflicted on oneself

Masturbation manual or instrumental stimulation of the genitalia, by oneself or another, to produce sexual satisfaction

Mattachine Society organization devoted to gay liberation

Mixoscopia deriving sexual satisfaction from watching other persons engaged in sexual activity; some brothels have either viewing windows or two-way mirrors and charge fee to persons desiring this activity

Morals squad vice squad

Narcissism exaggerated self-love

Narratophilia deriving principal sex satisfaction or stimulation from listening to sex stories

Necrophilia sexual fantasies about or overt sexual contact with dead bodies

Nymphomania compulsive, excessive desire for sexual intercourse in female

Obscenity material dealing with the genitalia, excremental functions, or with the sex process, dominated by prurient interests, and not acceptable by large numbers of people in society

Oedipus complex compulsive, excessive though usually unconscious sexual interest in mother by son

Orgasm physiological reaction that takes place in male or female upon achievement of maximum sexual satisfaction; climax; in male, usually accompanied by ejaculation

PG parental guidance; rating given a film with explicit sexual language or matter; but short of hard-core pornography

Pandering pimping, procuring

Pedomania compulsive sex drive toward boys

Perversion, sexual generic term for criminal, disvalued, socially unacceptable sex behaviors, sex aberrations, sex deviations; generally used pejoratively, but sometimes in a more neutral manner to describe any deflection of the sex drive from heterosexual intercourse

Pervert a person who attempts, practices, or harbors interest in the practice of sex perversions

Picacism, sexual heterosexual aberrations, anomalies, deviances

Pictophilia deriving principal sexual satisfaction from erotic pictures of nude paintings, drawings, etc.

Pimp one who offers prostitutes to others; one who recruits, manages, and shares the earnings of prostitutes

Pornography written or pictoral material with overt sexual portrayal in a manner generally unacceptable in a society

Promiscuity indiscriminate or near discriminate sex behavior with wide variety of partners, usually but not necessarily all of one sex

Prostitution sale of the body for sexual purpose to others for a fee, usually indiscriminately or nearly so

Prurience lasciviousness, lewdness

Public indecency indecent exposure or lewd and lascivious conduct in public; may consist of public urination, fellatio, copulation, or other act

Public morals, crimes against generic classification for most sex crimes, as prostitution, sodomy, but usually not including forcible rape, which is classified as crime against the peson

Pyromania pathological fire setting, said to be frequently sexually motivated

Queen effeminate male homosexual

Queer homosexual (adj. or noun)

R restricted; rating for moving pictures containing sexually oriented diaglogue or situations, but not hard-core-pornography; children under 16-17 not admitted

Rape, forcible sexual intercourse with an unwilling female by force or threat of force

Rape, sodomistic anal intercourse accomplished on man or woman by force or threat of serious injury

Rape, statutory consensual sexual intercourse between a male and a female, when the former is over and the latter under the age of consent;in some states, term applies when there is a custodial-patient or custodial-inmate relationship

Ravish rape

Redeeming social value standard set up by Supreme Court for judgment of pornography and obscenity cases: "...utterly without redeeming social values"

Red light district section of a community in which prostitution is permitted either by law or police policy.

Rubber contraceptive, condom

S & M (sadomasochism) behavior in which sexual satisfaction is obtained from inflicting pain or receiving pain; submission, flagellation, bondage and discipline

Satyr an extremely highly sexed male

Scoptophilia deriving sexual pleasure and satisfaction from looking at the sexual organs of others; homosexual scoptophiliacs often loiter in public toilets, lockers and shower rooms; hetersexuals often become voyeurs

Seduction act by which female permits intercourse only after a promise of male to marry her; her previous chastity was often considered sine qua non for act of seduction

Sex-abuse masturbation

Sex-aberration any of the sexual deviations or perversions; sexual anomaly, paraphilia

Sex-murder lust murder

Sex psycopath legal term used in sex psycopath laws to classify those charged with certain sex-related offenses

Sexual assault uninvited touching of the genitals, buttocks, or breasts of another; indecent assault

Short eyes prison jargon for someone incarcerated for carnal abuse of minor or child molestation; from shorties

Sodomy anal intercourse, but often used to include all oral-genital relations, bestiality, and other acts

Solicitation (for immoral purpose) police-prosecutorial term for making an approach to potential sex customers by male or female prostitutes; also applied to approaches by males to other males for nonprostitutive sex

Streaking running nude in public places

Streetwalking solicitation for prostitution on a public street or thoroughfare

Stud virile male

Syphilis venereal disease

Trade male with exaggerated masculine demeanor, who makes himself available to passive homosexuals for fellatio, particularly for money; also used for heterosexual male of similar demeanor

Unnatural act sexual aberrations and/or deviations

VD venereal disease

Vice squad police unit in charge of violations of laws relating to prostitution

Victimless crimes consensual acts, sexual and other, in which there is no complainant, no victim except a willing adult participant, and on which there is no agreement in society that they are harmful modes of behavior

Voyeur one deriving sexual satisfaction from viewing others in the nude, undressing, or in act of copulation, or by attending live sex shows or pornographic films; peeping tom

Whore prostitute

X rated XX rated rating applied to hard-core pornographic films depicting sexuality, and especially sex aberrations

Zooeroticism deriving or seeking sexual satisfaction from relationships with animals

Table 1A

Printing, Sale, Public Display, Distribution, etc., of Obscene Literature, Pictures, etc., Including Statutes Directed at Comic Books

State	Citation	Penalty
Alabama	T14 §373 T14 §374	$1000 $500
Alaska	§§65-9-11a to 11d	$300 a/o 30D
Arizona	13-532	$300 a/o 6M
Arkansas	§41-2702 §41-2704	$250 a/o 1Y 1: $500 a/o 60D; 2: $1000 & 6M; 3: 3Y
	§§41-2707, 2708	$100
California	PC §311	$500 a/o 6M
Colorado	§§60-9-16, 17	$2000 and 1Y
Connecticut	§53-243 §53-244	$1000 a/o 2Y Anti Comic book; $500 a/o 6M

Table 1B

Theatrical Obscenity, Including Motion Pictures, Carnivals, Dance Halls, Liquor Establishments and Statutes Respecting Obscene Exhibition of Children

State	Seach & Seizure	Citation	Penalty
Alabama			
Alaska		§65-9-6	$500 or 1Y
Arizona	§18-533		
Arkansas		§§41-1103, 1106	Exhibition of children: 1: $100 a/o 3M; 2: $200 or 6M
California	PC §312	Labor §§1308, 1309	$250 a/o 6M
Colorado	§40-9-19 §40-9-22 (injunction)		
Connecticut	§§54-29, -30	§53-25 §53-245 §22-121 §22-123	Exhibition of children: $250 a/o 1Y $1000 a/o 1Y Lease void Prohibited at agricultural fairs; penalty: 1: $50; 2: $50 and 30D; 3: $100 and 60D

State	Citation	Penalty	Seach & Seizure	Citation	Penalty
				§29-117	Motion pictures: $1000 a/o 1Y
				§§29-129,-130	Amusement parks: commissioner may require information in licensing to protect public from obscenity
Delaware	T11 §§711, 712	1: $2500 a/o 3Y; 2: $5000 a/o 5Y		T4 §561(5)	Ground for revoking liquor license
	T11 §435	$100		T11 §432	$100
D.C.	§22-2001	$500 a/o 1Y		§22-2001	$500 a/o 1Y
Florida	§847.01(1) §847.01(2)	$2000 a/o 5Y 5Y in pen or 1Y in county jail or $2000	§847.01 (7, 8) §847.02 §847.03 §847.06 §933.03	§450.151	Exhibition of children: $500 or 6M
	§847.06	$500 a/o 1Y			
Georgia	§26.6301 §26-6305 §§26-6301a to 6307a	5Y Same State literature commission		§54-9903	Exhibition of children: $1000 a/o 12M
Hawaii	§267-8	$500 or 6M	§267-9	§§277-1 to -3	Disorderly houses: $100 or 6M
				§309-26	Soliciting for: $500 a/o 1Y
Idaho	§18-4101 §§18-1506 to 1510	$300 a/o 6M Anti comic-book; $500 a/o 6M	§18-4102	§18-4101(5) §44-1306	Exhibition of children: $250 a/o 6M
Illinois	c.38 §§ 106 to 108	$500 a/o 6M	c.38 §692	c.38 §§92 to 94, 96	Exhibition of children: 1: $100 a/o 3M; 2: $500 a/o 2Y

78

State	Statute	Penalty	Statute	Note / Penalty
	c.38 §§468, 469	$1000 or 6M	c.38 §121b	No obscenity a condition of carnival permit, violation: $200
	c.38 §472a	$100	c.38 §151f	Immoral practices a ground for revocation of dance hall permit
	c.24 §§23-56	Prohibition is among powers of municipal corporation	c.38 §159(a) / c.38 §470	$1000 a/o 6M / 1: $200 a/o 1Y, / 2: $500 a/o 2Y
			c.38 §471	Group libel: $200
Indiana	§§10-2803 to 2805	$1000 a/o 1Y	§9-601 / §§9-604 to 606	
	§§10-4704, 4705		§10-808	Exhibition of children: $100 and discretionary 30D
			§15-221	State fair board not to permit obscene shows
Iowa	§725.4 / §725.5 / §725.6 / §725.8	$1000 or 1Y / $1000 a/o 1Y / Same / Comic books; $50 a/o 6M	§225.9	
	§725.11	$1000 or 1Y	§725.3	$1000 a/o 1Y
Kansas	§21-1101 / §21-1102	$1000 a/o 6M / $300 a/o 30D / 5Y		
	§§21-1103, 1104	$100 a/o 1Y	§38-705 / §§51-101 to 112	2Y / Provision for motion picture censor board; penalty for exhibiting unapproved or indecent films: $50 or 30D
	§§21-1105, 1106			
	§§21-1115 to 1118	$50 a/o 30D	§51-112 (films only)	
Kentucky	§§436.090 to .110	$1000 a/o 1Y	§436.570 (injunction)	
	§436.550 / §436.560	Same / $500 a/o 6M	§199.340	Exhibition of children: 1: $20 a/o 90D; 2: $100 a/o 1Y
Louisiana	c.14 §106(2)	$2000 a/o 5Y	c.15 §43(1)	
			c.14 §106(3) / c.14 §281 / c.23 §251(4)	$2000 a/o 5Y / $100 a/o 90D / Exhibition of children: $250 a/o 2Y

State	Citation	Penalty	Seach & Seizure	Citation	Penalty
Maine	c.134 §24 c.134 §27	$50 or 30D $100 a/o 11M	c.134 §25	c.26 §§88(5), 285(5) c.134 §§28, 29 c.138 §8	Lewd or immoral entertainment: revocation of liquor license + $500 a/o 6M $500 a/o 11M Exhibition of children: $100 or 60D
Maryland	Art. 27 §417 Art. 27 §§418, 419 [§419 listed as invalidated by Winters v. New York, 333 U.S. 507 (1948)] Art. 27 §421B Art. 66A §15	$200 or 1Y $300 a/o 1Y invalidated by Winters v. New York, 333 U.S. 507 (1948)] $200 a/o 6M (comic books) Exhibition of obscene advertisements for movies; penalty: revocation of license for film		Art. 27 §419B Art. 66A	$200 a/o 1Y Motion picture censorship act; penalty for violation: 1: $50; 2: $100; in default of payment of either: 30D (§20)
Massachusetts	c.272 §28 c.272 §§ 28A, 28B c.272 §§28C to 28H c.272 §30	1: $1000 a/o 2Y; 2: $2000 a/o 30M; $1000 a/o 2Y Procedure for having books declared obscene $1000 or 2Y	c.276 §18(8) c.276 §7	c.272 §§31, 32	$500 a/o 1Y
Michigan	§§28.575 (1-3) §28.576 §28.577 §§27.1410 (1 to 10)	$100 a/o 90D $1000 a/o 1Y Comic books: $100 a/o 9OD $100 a/o 9OD Proceedings relating to sale or distribution of obscene literature, etc.	§27.1410(5) §28.578	§28.335	Exhibition of children: $500 or 1Y

State					
Minnesota	§617.24 §617.25 §617.243	$500 a/o 1Y $100 or 3M $1000 or 1Y	§617.27 §626.02(2)		At state fair: $100 a/o 3M At dance halls: revocation of license + $100 or 3M
Mississippi	§2280 §2288	$100 a/o 30D $500 a/o 6M		§2286 §10223	Motion pictures: $100 a/o 60D Unlawful for holder of liquor permit: $500 a/o 6M + revoke or suspend permit
Missouri	§563.270	Not less than $100 a/o more than 1Y	§542.380(2)		
	§563.280 §563.290 §563.310	$1000 a/o 1Y Same Comic books: $100 a/o 6M			
Montana	§94-3603(3-5) §94-3601	$500 a/o 6M Same	§§94-3604 to 3606	§94-3603(5)	Lewd songs: $500 a/o 6M
Nebraska	§§28-921,922	$1000 a/o 1Y	§28-925 §29-801(4)	§§28-1120, 1121	$100 a/o 90D
	§28-924	Comic books: $500 a/o 6M			
Nevada	§201.250	$500 a/o 6M		§609.210	Exhibition of children: $500 a/o 6M
New Hampshire	§§571:14 to 18	$500 a/o 6M			
New Jersey	§2A:115-2,_3	$1000 a/o 3Y	§2A:152-5		
	§2A:115-3.1	Person forcing tie-in is a disorderly person: penalty: $1000 a/o 1Y			

State	Citation	Penalty	Search & Seizure	Citation	Penalty
N. J. (Cont.)	§2A:115-3.2	$2000 a/o 7Y			
New Mexico					
New York	Penal §1141	1: $2000 a/o 1Y; 2: $3000 a/o 1Y; 3: $5000 a/o 3Y	Penal §1141-c Penal §1144 CCP §22-a (injunction against sale)	Penal §1140-a Penal §1141	Revocation of license 1: $2000 a/o 1Y; 2: $3000 a/o 1Y; 3: $5000 a/o 3Y
	Penal §§1141-a,-b	$500 a/o 1Y		CCP §552	Above not bailable where defendant has two prior convictions of certain misdemeanors or a conviction of any felony
	Penal §1143 CCP §552	Same All above not bailable where defendant has two prior convictions of certain misdemeanors or of any felony		Penal §485-a(5)	Exhibition of children: $50 a/o 1Y; 1: $100; 2: $200 ($99)
				Agriculture & Market Law §288	
				Education Law §120 Education Law §129	Motion picture licensing Exhibition of unlicensed film: $500 a/o 1Y
North Carolina	§14-189 §14-189.1 §14-194	Misdemeanor° Misdemeanor° Misdemeanor°		§§14-189.1, -190, §14-193	Misdemeanor° Motion pictures: Misdemeanor°
				§14-198	Lewd women within 3 miles of schools: $50 or 30D
	°Misdemeanor punishable in discretion of court			°Misdemeanor punishable in discretion of court	
North Dakota	§12-2107 §12-2109 §12-2110(3)	$1000 a/o 1Y Same $500 a/o 1Y	§12-2111 §2-2112 §2-2113	§12-2110(2) §53-0303	$500 a/o 1Y Permit to conduct carnival granted on condition no lewd shows presented; penalty: $500 a/o 90D

State					
Ohio	§2903.10	Comic books: $100 a/o 6M	§2905.35, §2933.21(D), §2905.343 (injunction against sale)	§2905.342, §2905.40, §2905.41	$1000 a/o 6M; 1: $500; 2: $500 & 6M; In saloons: $100 a/o 30D
	§2905.34, §2905.341, §2905.37, §§3767.01 to .11	$2000 a/o 7Y; $1000 a/o 6M; Definition of "obscene"; Abatement as nuisance of manufacturer or obscene slides, films		§§3767.01 to .11	Abatement of, as nuisance
	§715.54	Municipal corporation may restrain or prohibit			
Oklahoma	T21 §1021(3,4); T21 §§1040.1 to .7	$1000 a/o 10Y to Literature commission	T21 §§1022 to 1024; T21 §§1032 to 1039 (injunction against sale)	T11 §655	City councils may restrain, prohibit
	T21 §1035			T21 §1021	$1000 a/o 10Y
Oregon	§167.150, §167.152	$500 a/o 6M; $500 a/o 1Y		§167.145, §167.150(5)	$500 or 1Y; $500 a/o 1Y
Pennsylvania	T18 §§3831 to 3833	$500 a/o 1Y	T18 §783 [repealed? See T18 §5201]	T4 §§70.1 to .14; T4 §70.10; T4 §70.18	Board of Motion Picture Control; Injunction against movies; Penalty: $1000 a/o 6M
	T18 §4524, T18 §4530	$2000 a/o 2Y; $500 a/o 1Y	T18 §3832.1 (injunction)	T18 §4528	$1500 a/o 2Y
Puerto Rico	T33 §1171(3)	$250 a/o 2Y	T33 §§1172 to 1174	T33 §1171(2)	$250 a/o 2Y

State	Citation	Penalty	Search & Seizure	Citation	Penalty
Rhode Island	§11-31-1 §11-31-9 §11-31-10 §11-31-12	$2000 or 2Y Comic books: $1000 2Y a/o 2Y $2000 or 2Y	§§11-31-2 to 8 §11-31-13 (injunction)	§§11-31-3, -4 §11-31-5	$500 a/o 1Y Seizure of instruments used for obscene shows
South Carolina	§16-414	$1000 a/o 2Y	§16-414.1 (injunction)		
South Dakota	§13.1722(3,-4)	$500 a/o 1Y	§13.1723	§13.1722(2) §13.1722(3, 4)	$500 a/o 1Y Movies: Same Exhibition of children: 1: $100 a/o 30D; 2: $200 or 6M
Tennessee	§39-3001	$1000 a/o 1Y		§6-202	Municipality can prevent
Texas	PC Art. 526 PC Arts. 527 to 527b	$100 $1000 a/o 6M		PC Art. 516	Employment of prostitutes in theater: $500 and 20D for each day such woman is kept in service
				PC Art. 527 PC Art. 532 PC Art. 612	Movies: $1000 a/o 6M Women's dance troups: $500 and 1Y $1000 a/o 60D
Utah	§76-39-1(3)	$300 a/o 6M	§§76-39-2 to 4	§76-39-1 (2, 5)	$300 a/o 6M
Vermont	T13 §2801 T13 §2802 T13 §2804 T13 §2805	$200 a/o 1Y $200 or 3M $200 or 1Y Comic books: $100	T13 §§4701 to 4703	T13 §§2802, 2803	$200 a/o 3M
Virginia	§18.1-228 §18.1-231,232 §§18.1-233 to 235	$500 a/o 12M Same 1: $500 a/o 12M 2: $2000 or 2Y	§19.1-84	§§18.1-228, -229 §18.1-230 §18.1-235	Movies: $500 a/o 12M $500 a/o 12M Slides, movies: 1: $500 a/o 12M; 2: $2000 or 2Y

State					
Washington	§9.68.010, .020 c. 19.18	$250 or 90D Licensing comic book dealers	c7.42 (injunctions)	§9.68.010(4) §67.12.040	$250 or 90D In dance halls: $250 a/o 90D
	§§29.79.360, 29.80.030	Relate to content of election pamphlets			
West Virginia	§6066	1: $1000 and 1Y 2: 5Y	§6164		
	§494	Municipalities can arrest and convict persons for			
	Constitution Art. 3, §7	Exception to freedom of speech for			
	§2666(2)	For violation of §6066, discretionary sex offender inquiry			
Wisconsin	§944.21 §944.22 §944.23	$5000 a/o 5Y $1000 a/o 1Y $100 a/o 60D	§962.02(3) §963.04(5)	§944.21(d)	$5000 a/o 5Y
			§269.565 (declaratory judgments)		
Wyoming	§§6-103.104	$100 and discretionary 6M	§7-148		
				§27-232	Exhibition of children: $100 a/o 90D
				§27-235	Exhibition of children: $1000 a/o 12M

Table 1C
Wall Obscenity

State	Citation	Penalty
Alabama		
Alaska		
Arizona		
Arkansas		
California	T14 §872	$500 or 12M
Colorado		
Connecticut		
Delaware		
D.C.		
Florida	§450.091	Toilets provided laborers to be kept free from: $500 a/o 6M
Georgia	§235.09	$100 or 15D
Hawaii	§26-6302	5Y
Idaho		
Illinois		
Indiana		

Table 1D
Obscene Advertising

State	Citation	Penalty
Alabama		
Alaska		
Arizona		
California	B&P §600	$500 a/o 1Y
	B&P §601	5Y
	B&P §4322	$500 a/o 6M
	B&P §5290	Same
Colorado	§40-9-26	$300 a/o 6M
Connecticut	§19-233	$500 a/o 6M; if violation committed after a conviction final: $1000 a/o 1Y
Delaware		
D.C.		
Florida	T16 §2502	$100
	§500.19	$500 or 6M; if violation committed after a conviction final: $1000 or 1Y
	§797.02	$1000 or 1Y
Georgia	§51-19(b)	$500 a/o 1Y
Hawaii	§60-9	Chiropractor's license revoked
Idaho	§154-14	$500 a/o 1M
	§155-73	$250
	§18-603	$5000 a/o 5Y
	§§39-701 to 704	$500 a/o 6M
	§39-807	$300 a/o 6M+suspend pharmacy license
Illinois	c.38 §6	$1000 or 3Y
Indiana	§10-2803	$1000 and discretionary 1Y

State			Citation	Penalty
Iowa	§88.2		§10-2806	$500 and discretionary 6M; 1: $1000 a/o 6M; 2: $2000 a/o 2Y; $1000 a/o 1Y
Kansas			§35-3107	$1000 a/o 6M
Kentucky			§§725.5, .7	$500 a/o 1Y
Louisiana		Toilets provided laborers to be kept free from: $10	§21-1101; §436.090	$500 a/o 6M; $100 or 3M
Maine	c.41 §234		c.14 §88; c.134 §11; c.134 §26; Art. 27 §3	$100 a/o 3M; $1000 a/o not less than 3Y
Maryland		$10	Art. 66A §15	Obscene advertisements for movies; penalty: revocation of license for film 3Y prison or 2Y jail or $1000
Massachusetts			c.272 §20	
Michigan	§28.227	$100 a/o 90D	c.272 §29; §28.205; §28.223 to 226	$500 a/o 6M; $100 a/o 90D; Same
Minnesota			§28.229	$500 a/o 1Y
Mississippi	§2049	On walls of capitol: $500 a/o 6M	§617.25; §617.28; §2289; §4227-02(a)	$500 or 6M; $200 and 3M; Trade marks not to contain "immoral matter"
Missouri			§563.300	$1000 a/o 6M
Montana			§§94-3609; §§94-3611, 3612; §94-3617	$500 a/o 6M; Same
Nebraska			§28-923; §201.430	$1000 a/o 1Y; 1: $50; 2: $250
Nevada			§201.440; §§202.190 to .200; §202.240	1: $100; 2: $250; $3000 a/o 1Y
New Hampshire	§507:3			$500 a/o 6M
New Jersey				
New Mexico		$25 a/o 6M		

State				
New York			Penal §1142	1: $2000 a/o Y; 2: $3000 a/o 1Y; 3: $5000 a/o 3Y
			Penal §1142-a CCP §552	Above not bailable where defendant has two prior convictions of certain misdemeanors or of any felony. For movies: $500 a/o 1Y
North Carolina	§14-192	$50 or 30D	Educ. §130	(Movies) Misdemeanor or punishable in discretion of court
North Dakota			§14-193	
Ohio			§2905.33 §2905.34 §2905.38 §2905.39	$1000 a/o 6M / $2000 a/o 7Y / $100 a/o 100D / 1: $500; 2: $500 and 6M
Oklahoma				
Oregon			§167.150(2)	$500 a/o 6M
Pennsylvania	T18 §4527 T43 §109	$500 a/o 1Y; Toilets provided laborers to be kept free from: $500 a/o 60D	T18 §4525 T18 §4526 T18 §4529 T18 §4531	$500 a/o 1Y / Same / $300 a/o 6M / $500 a/o 1Y
Puerto Rico Rhode Island South Carolina South Dakota			T10 §§315, 316	$100
			§16-415 §13.1726	$1000 a/o 2Y / $100 a/o 30D+revoke any license
Tennessee Texas Utah Vermont	T13 §3701	$20 a/o 90D	PC Art. 702 §76-39-1(4) T13 §104 T13 §305	$200 / $300 a/o 6M / 10Y / $100 a/o 1Y
Virginia Washington			§18.1-232 §§9.04.030, .040 §9.68.030	$500 a/o 12M / $1000 a/o 1Y / $250 or 90D
West Virginia Wisconsin Wyoming	§21-86	$100	§§6-103 to 105	$100 and discretionary 6M

Table 2A
OBSCENE LANGUAGE IN PUBLIC

Table 2B
OBSCENITY

	Citation	Penalty	IN PRESENCE OF WOMEN (a)		NEAR DWELLING (b)	
			Citation	Penalty	Citation	Penalty
Alabama			T14 §§11, 116	$200 and discretionary 6M	T14 §11	$200 and discretionary 6M
Alaska						
Arizona	§13-377 §13-378	$50 or 2M Lewd songs; $300 a/o 6M	§13-377	$50 or 2M		
Arkansas	§41-1401 §41-1416	$300 a/o 6M $50			§41-1415	$200
California	PC §311 (5, 6)	$500 a/o 6M	PC §415 B&P §7700	$200 a/o 90D Funeral director's obscenity in presence of family a ground for discipline		
Colorado						
Connecticut						
Delaware						
D.C.	§22-1107	$250 a/o 90D				
Florida	§232.26	Pupil may be suspended for obscene language			§847.04	$25 or 60D
	§352.02	Conductor may eject passenger				
	§847.04	$25 or 60D				
	§847.05	$25 or 30D				

89

			(a) IN PRESENCE OF WOMEN		(b) NEAR DWELLING	
	Citation	Penalty	Citation	Penalty	Citation	Penalty
Georgia	§26-6303	$1000 a/o 12M	§26-6303	$1000 a/o 12M		
Hawaii	§302-1	$20 or 1M				
Idaho			§18-6409	$300 a/o 6M		
Illinois	c38 §175	Disturbing religious meetings: $100				
	c114 §87	Conductor may eject passenger				
Indiana	§10-2801	$100 a/o 6M	§10-2801	$100 and discretionary 6M		
Iowa	§477.56	Obscenity on trains				
	§477.57	Obscenity on trains; conductor may eject passenger				
	§728.1	$100 or 30D				
	§744.2	Disturbing religious meetings: same				
Kansas	§21-949	Disturbing religious meetings: $100 or 3M				
Kentucky	§§277.260, .990 (6)	Conductor may eject passenger, passenger liable to $100 a/o 50D				
	§437.090	In street cars: $10				

State					
Louisiana	§106 (3 to 5)	$500 a/o 2Y	c14 §92/6, 7)	Contributing to delinquency: $500 a/o 1Y	
Maine	c137 §41	Vagabondage: 90D			
Maryland				See Art. 27 §124	$25
Massachusetts	c272 §43 c272 §59	On trains, etc.: $50 Person using obscenity can be arrested without warrant	c112 §84	Embalmer's obscenity a ground for suspension	
Michigan	§22.268 §§28.634, .365	Conductor may eject passenger Disorderly person: 1: $100 or 3M; 2: $100 a/o 3M; 3: $100 or 2Y	§28.569	$100 a/o 90D	
Minnesota	§615.12 §617.47	On public conveyance: $100 or 3M In dance halls: same		§615.15	In presence of Family $100 or 3M
Mississippi	§2291 §7156 §7788 §7791	$200 Hotel may eject guest $100 a/o 30D Conductor may eject passenger	§2089	Misdemeanor	§2089 Misdemeanor
Missouri					
Montana	§94-3603 (5)	$500 a/o 6M			
Nebraska	§§15-256, 16-228	Powers of municipalities	§28-920	$100 or 90D	
Nevada	§201.270 (1)	Disturbing religious services: $500 a/o 6M			

Table 2A (Con't)   Table 2B (Con't)

| | | IN PRESENCE OF WOMEN (a) | | NEAR DWELLING (b) |
Citation	Penalty	Citation	Penalty	Citation
§266.350 (5)	City council may punish			
New Hampshire §§570:1, :3 §570.18	$25 a/o 6M On public conveyances: same $100 a/o 6M			
§570.25 §578.6	Disturbing services: $10 a/o 30D City council can punish			
§47:17 (XIII)				
New Jersey §2A:170-29	Disorderly person: $1000 a/o 1Y			
§18:1-26	On state lands: $150			
New Mexico				
New York Penal §§2071, 2072	Disturbing religious meetings: $500 a/o 1Y			
Town Law §130 (11)	Town can prohibit			
North Carolina §14-195	On public conveyance: $50 or 30D	§§14-196,-196.1	Misdemeanor punished in discretion of court	
§14-197	$50 or 30D			

92

State				
North Dakota	§12-2106 §12-2125 §12-4204 (5)	$100 a/o 30D Disturbing religious meetings $500 a/o 1Y Vagrancy: $100 a/o 30D	$12-2106	$100 a/o 30D
Ohio	§715.55 §4951.57	Municipal corporation may punish On streetcar: $10	$2905.30	$200 a/o 6M
Oklahoma	T21 §906 T21 §1362	$100 a/o 30D Same	T21 §906	$100 a/o 30D
Oregon	§166.080(f) §166.120	Vagrancy: $100 a/o 6M Disturbing religious meetings: $200 a/o 6M		
Pennsylvania	§§167.155, .160 T53 §22266	$500 a/o 6M Police magistrates in cities of second class have jurisdiction over		
Puerto Rico	T33 §1171(5)	$250 a/o 2Y		
Rhode Island	§11-45-1	Vagrancy: 3Y in correctional institution		
South Carolina	§16-557 §16-558 §15-909	Disturbing religious meetings: $100 a/o 1Y Misdemeanor Guardhouse or chain gang for not more than 30D (municipal court act)	See §16-552	Lewd letters: punished in discretion of court

93

State				
	§47-150	Same, powers of municipalities under 1000 pop.		
	§47-234	Commission to guardhouse, not to exceed 24 hours, before trial (powers of municipalities under 1000 pop.)		
	§58-1222	Conductor may eject passenger		
South Dakota	§13.1704(1)	Disturbing religious meetings: $500 a/o 1Y	§13.1708	$100 a/o 30D
	§13.1708	$100 a/o 30D		
Tennessee				
Texas	PC Art. 474 Art. 5154(d)(2)	$200 $500 a/o 90D (in picketing)		
Utah	§76-39-1(5)	$300 a/o 6M		
Vermont				
Virginia				
Washington	§9.68.040	$250 or 90D		
West Virginia	§591(63)	Home rule cities have power to suppress		
Wisconsin				
Wyoming		§6-102		$100 and discretionary 3M

Table 2C

	(a) Lewd Letters		(b) Obscenity over Telephone	
	Citation	Penalty	Citation	Penalty
Alabama				
Alaska				
Arizona				
Arkansas				
California				
Colorado				
Connecticut			T 11 §758	$200 a/o 1Y
Delaware				
District of Columbia				
Florida				
Georgia	§26-6303	$1000 a/o 12M	§302-2	$100 or 3M
Hawaii	See §267-8 (defamatory letters, general)	$500 or 6M		
Idaho				
Illinois				
Indiana			§10-1511	$500 a/o 6M
Iowa				
Kansas				
Kentucky				
Louisiana			c.14 §285	$5000 a/o 2Y
Maine				
Maryland				
Massachusetts				
Michigan				
Minnesota				

95

State	Citation	Penalty	Citation	Penalty
Mississippi				
Missouri				
Montana				
Nebraska				
Nevada	§207.180	$500 and 6M	§2281.5	$500 a/o 6M
New Hampshire				
New Jersey	§2A:115.4 (to women)	$1000 a/o 3Y	§2A:170-29(3)	Disorderly person $1000 a/o 1Y
New Mexico				
New York			Penal §555	$500 a/o 1Y
North Carolina			§14-196 (to telephone operator)	Misdemeanor punished in discretion of court
			§14-196.1 (to women)	Same
			§14-196.2 (to anyone)	Same
North Dakota			§12-2106	$100 a/o 30D
Ohio				
Oklahoma				
Oregon				
Pennsylvania			T 18 §4414.1	$500 to which may be added 6M
Puerto Rico				
Rhode Island				
South Carolina	§16-552 (to women)	Discretion of court		
South Dakota				
Tennessee			§39-3002	$1000 and discretionary
Texas			PC Art. 476	$100
Utah				
Vermont				
Virginia			§18.1-238	$500 a/o 12M
Washington				
West Virginia				
Wisconsin			§6071	$100
Wyoming				

Table 3
RAPE

	Forcible	Unconscious Victim	Drugged Victim	Mentally Ill Victim	Deceived Victim (Incl. Impersonation of husband)
Ala.	T14 §395 Death or not less than 1OY		T14 §397 same		T14 §400 same T14 §41 attempt: $500 and discretionary 12M
Alaska	§65-4-12 §65-4-13 **20Y** §65-4-16 (AWITC) 15Y				
Ariz.	§13-611 Life			X	X
Ark.	§§41-3401 to 3403 Death or life §41-3404 Accesory: 21Y		§41-3405 same		
Cal.	§41-607 (AWITC) °1Y PC §§261, 264 Not less than 3Y PC §220 (AWITC) 20Y PC §653f (soliciting a person to commit $5000 or 5Y PC §2670 ("asexualization" for 3-time recidivist of rape or AWITC) PC §1203 (no probation) PC §11112 (fingerprinting)	X		X	X
Colorado	§40-2-25 Life		Administered without victim's knowledge: life; if with her knowledge and she is over 18: 10Y	Life	If fraud: life; if victim under 18 and impersonate husband: 10Y

	Forcible	Unconscious Victim	Drugged Victim	Mentally Ill Victim	Deceived Victim (incl.) Impersonation of Husband
Conn.	§40-2-34 (AWITC) 5Y §39-10-18 (loss of civil rights) §53-202 10Y §53-238 30Y			§53-225 3Y	
Delaware	T11 §781 Life T11 §782 (AWITC) 10Y $50 and 10Y and 30 lashes				
D.C.	§22-2801 30Y or death in discretion of jury				
Fla.	§794.01 Death, or life if jury recommends			§794.06 10Y	
Georgia	§26-1302 Death, or if jury recommend mercy, 20Y				
Hawaii	§309-31 Life §309-16 AWITC: $100 and Life				
Idaho	§§18-6101 to 6104 Life §18-907 (AWITC) 14Y	X		X	X
Ill.	c38 §490 Life c38 §587 Person convicted is infamous, disabled from holding office, voting jury service, unless pardoned or otherwise restored according to law c38 §58 AWITC 14Y c38 §84 Burglary WITC: life c38 §85 Attempt at §84: 5Y c38 §86 In building WITC: 5Y c38 §602 Second offense: not less than 15Y (habitual offender act) c38 §785 No probation c108 §106 Special confinement where incestuous				
Ind.	§10-4201 21Y, but if victim is under 12,				

State					
Iowa	life mandatory §10-4709 (armed) 20Y	§698.1 Life §698.14 AWITC 20Y §247.20 Court cannot parole	§698.3 same		§10-4203 Female defendant; male victim 21Y §698.3 same
Kansas		§21-424 21Y	§21-425 Victim 18 & up: same		
Kentucky		§435.090 Death or not less than 20Y			
Louisiana		c14 §42 Death only c29 §42 court martial c15 §529.2 Persons convicted not to be put in "prison districts"	c14 §43 20Y	c14 §43 20Y	c14 §43 20Y	c14 §43 20Y
Maine		c130 §10 Any term c130 §12 AWITC 500 or 10Y			
Md.		Art 27 §§461, 463: Court may sentence defendant to death, life, or to a term not more than 21 Y; but if jury return verdict "without capital punishment" court cannot sentence defendant to more than 20Y Art 27 §12 AWITC: death			Art 27 §462 same
Mass.		c265 §22 Life c265 §22A Victim under 16 (forcible): life; if defendant over 21 and second offense: not less than 5Y c265 §24 AWITC: life	c272 §3 $1000 a/o 3Y c94 §217C (narcotics) 1: $10,000 and 15Y; 2: $10,-000 and 20Y; 3: $10,000 and 30Y		c272 §5 $1000 a/o 3Y

	Forcible	Unconscious Victim	Drugged Victim	Mentally Ill Victim	Deceived Victim (incl.) Impersonation of Husband
Mich.	§28.788 Life or any term of years or indeterminate sentence 1D to life if found to be "sexually delinquent person" (§28.200[1]) §28.280 AWITC: $5000 or 10Y or indeterminate sentence as above	X		§28.573 Patient in insane asylum: 15Y	
Minn.	§617.01 30Y		X	X	
Miss.	§2358 Death or life if jury so determine §2011 AWITC $1000 a/o 1Y §2361 AWITC on chaste victim: life, or less if jury so determine	X	X	§6782 $1000 a/o 1Y	
Mo.	§559.260 Death or not less than 2Y in discretion of jury §559.180 AWIT ravish: not less than 2Y §559.190 AWIT rape: 5Y in pen or not less than 6M in county jail or not less than $100 and not less than 3M in county jail or not less than $100 §559.470 Loss of "citizenship" (applies to §§559.180, .260, .270) §549.080 Parole not to be given by court		§559.270 Not less than 5Y		X
Mont.	§94-4101 99Y		X		
Nebr.	§28-408 20Y §28-407 (incestuous) life §28-409 AWITC 15Y §83-504 Castration on order of court §29-2217 No probation Note: provision in §29-2620 for indeterminate sentence held not available in rape, Laison v. State, 125 Neb. 789, 252 N.W. 195			§28-901 10Y §83-504 (Col. 1)	

Nev.	§200.360 5Y to death; if extreme violence, 20Y to death in discretion of jury		
	§200.400 AWITC: 14Y; if with extreme cruelty and great bodily injury, 14Y to death in jury's discretion		
	§207.020 Court may order sterilization in addition to any other penalty		
N. H.	§585:16 30Y		
	§583:1 Burglary WITC: 25Y		
	§173:3 Sexual psychopath inquiry mandatory		
N. J.	§2A:138-1 $5000 a/o 30Y	X	§2A:138-A $1000 a/o 3Y
	§2A:90-2 AWITC, victim under 16: $3000 a/o 12Y		
	§2A:94-1 Breaking & entering WITC: $2000 a/o 7Y		
	§2A:98-2 No overt act necessary for conspiracy		
	§§2A:164-3 to 13: Mandatory commitment to diagnostic center		
	§2A:164-28 Record not expunged in case of suspended sentence		
	§19:4-1 Denial of suffrage to person convicted of		
N. M.	§40-39-1 1 to 99Y	X	
	§40-6-9 AWITC 50Y		
N. Y.	Penal §2010 20Y or indeterminate life	X	
	Penal §1940 (second offense) indeterminate life	X	
	Penal §243 AWITC indeterminate life	X	
	Penal §1940 (second offense) (above)	X	

	Forcible	Unconscious Victim	Drugged Victim	Mentally Ill Victim	Deceived Victim (incl.) Impersonation of Husband
N. C.	§14-21 Death, unless jury recommend life §14-22 AWITC 15Y §14-6 Accessory before fact gets life §15-169 AWITC is lesser included offense				§14-24 20Y §14-25 15Y
N. D.	§12-30-04, -05 Defendant is 20 or older; not less than 1Y §§12-30-06, -07 defendant is 1Y; but less than 20: Same §12-30-08, -09 Defendant is under 17: 9Y in training school §12-30-12 Board of pardons may order psychiatric treatment		X		X
			X		X
			X		X
Ohio	§2905.01 20Y §2905.02 (incestuous) life is mandatory §2901.24 AWITC 15Y §2903.01 AWITC where defendant is under 18 and victim under 16: $1000 a/o 10Y §2951.04 No probation for rape or AWITC		See §2905.11 furnishing intoxicating drink to female WITC sexual intercourse: 3Y	§2905.06 Defendant over 17	
Okla.	T21 §§1111, 1114, 1115 Death or not less than 5Y		§1116 15Y	X	§1116 15Y

Ore.

§163.210 20Y
§163.220 (incestuous) life
§167.045 AWITC: same as for the greater crime
§167.045 Detention or enticement WITC: 5Y or life indeterminate
§167.050 Second offense of rape or incestuous rape, or prior violation of certain other crimes: indeterminate life
§137.111 Person convicted under any of §§163.210, .220, .270, or §167.045 may be sentenced to indeterminate life if victim is under 16
§137.112 Same as .111, psychiatric examination mandatory.

Penna.

T18 §4721 $7000 a/o 15Y solitary at hard labor
T18 §4722 AWITC $2000 a/o 5Y solitary
T19 §1166 AWITC indeterminate life
T19 §§1167 to 74 Psychiatric examination
T18 §5110 Where defendant over 21 has accomplice under 18, penalty may be doubled

P.R.

T33 §§961, 964 — X
Not less than 1Y
T33 §761 AWITC 14Y

R.I.

§11-37-1 — §11-37-4 5Y
not less than 10Y
§11-5-1 AWITC 20Y
§11-8-3 Entry WITC: $500 a/o 10Y

X (Ore.)
X (P.R.)

	Forcible	Unconscious Victim	Drugged Victim	Mentally Ill Victim	Deceived Victim (incl.) Impersonation of Husband
S.C.	§11-8-4 Same: 10Y §12-13-5 Only certain justices can bail 6M §12-13-6 Defendant can be held without bail §12-17-4 No peremptory challenges (so listed in index; not clear from section) §12-18-1 No probation by court §10-9-2 No habeas corpus §16-72 rape and AWITC: death unless jury designate mercy, in which case 40Y at hard labor §38-211 Double peremptory challenges Constitution Art. 2 §6 Conviction disqualifies elector				
S.D.	§§13.2801 to 2803: not less than 10Y	X 20Y	X 20Y	X not less than 10Y	X 20Y
Tenn.	§39-3702 Death, but jury may commute to not less than 10Y §39-605 AWITC 21Y §40-2712 Disenfranchisement		§30-3704 same		§39-3703 same
Texas	PC Art. 1189 death or not less than 5Y PC Art. 1162 AWITC: not less than 2Y PC Art. 1190 Attempt to rape not less than 2Y		PC Art. 1186 same	PC Art. 1183 same	PC Art. 1183 (fraud) same PC Art. 1186 (strategem) same

Table 4

STATUTORY RAPE

State				Penalties and provisions
Utah	X			§§76-53-15, -18 Not less than 10Y §76-7-7 AWITC 10Y §§77-49-1 to 8: presentence mental examination
Vt.				T13 §3201 $2000 a/o 20Y T13 §607 AWITC $1000 a/o 10Y
Va.		X	X	§18.1-44 Death or not less than 5Y §18.1-15 Conspiracy: 20Y
Wash.			X	§9.79.010 Not less than 5Y §§71.06.010 to .140 Post conviction or acquittal examination for sexual psychopathy
W. Va.				§5930 Death or life in court's discretion, or if jury recommend mercy, 5 to 20Y see §6065 Doctor or dentist administering anesthetic except in presence of third person: $100 a/o 60D §§2666(2)ff Discretionary sex offender examination
Wisc.				$944.02 15Y §944.01 30Y §939.66 Attempted battery is lesser included offense §959.15 Mandatory presentence mental examination and treatment
Wyo.				§6-63 Life §6-64 AWITC 50Y §§7-348 to 362 Presentence mental examination and treatment in lieu of penalty if defendant found to be within sex offender act

$944.02 15Y

$944.02 15Y

Table 4

STATUTORY RAPE

	Citation	Penalty	EXTRAORDINARY PENALTY WHERE VICTIM IS UNDER CERTAIN AGE (Forcible intercourse not distinguished) Citation & Penalty	
Alabama	T14§399	Victim under 16: 10Y; not applicable where defendant under 16	T14§398	Victim under 12: death or not less than 10Y
Alaska	§65-4-12	20Y		
	§65-4-13	Defendant under 19 and victim under 16: 20Y	§65-4-13	Defendant over 16 and victim under 12: any term of years
Arizona	§13-611(1)	Victim under 18: life		
	§13-615	Teacher and pupil: 10Y		
Arkansas	§41-3406	Victim under 16: 21Y		
California	PC§261(1)	50Y in pen or 1Y in county jail in jury's discretion; but if defendant pleads guilty, in court's discretion	PC§644	Habitual offender, victim under 14: life
			PC§645	Where victim under 10, sterilization is discretionary penalty
Colorado	§40-2-25 (1)	Where defendant is over 18 and victim under 18 offense is rape I: life		
	§40-2-25 (9)	Where both defendant and victim are under 18, offense is rape III: $1000 a/o 5Y; same penalty where male victim is under 18		
Connecticut	§53-238	Victim under 16: $1000 a/o 30Y		
	§53-240	Assault with intent to commit: 10Y		
	§40-9-7	Victim under 16: 10Y		
Delaware		Only age of consent is 7	T11§781	Victim under 7: life
District of Columbia	§22-2801	Victim under 16: 30Y (or death in discretion of jury)		
Florida	§794.05	Victim under 18: $2-000 or 10Y	§794.01	Victim under 10: death, or if jury recommend, life
Georgia	§§26-1303 to 1304	Victim under 14: same penalty as for rape except jury can recommend defendant be punished as for a misdemeanor		

106

	Citation	Penalty	EXTRAORDINARY PENALTY CERTAIN AGE (Forcible intercourse not distinguished) Citation & Penalty
Hawaii	§309-14	Victim under 16: 10Y	§309-20 §309-16 — Victim under 12: life Assault with intent to der 12: $1000 and commit, victim un- life at hard labor
Idaho	§§18-6101 to 6104	Victim under 18: life (or less in discre- tion of court)	
Illinois	c38§490	Defendant 17 & up; victim under 16 life.	
	c38§587	Person convicted is "i n f a m o u s" and suffers certain dis- abilities, as to which see table on rape	
	c38§602	Second offense: not less than 15Y (ha- bitual offender act)	
	c108§106	Confinement in spe- cial division of prison	
Indiana	§10-4201	Victim under 16: 21Y	§10-4201 — Victim under 12: life
Iowa	§698.1	Victim under 16; or defendant over 25 and victim under 17, life.	
	§698.4	Assault with intent to commit: 20Y	
Kansas	§21-424 §21-909	21Y Guardian and ward: 21Y	
Kentucky	§435.100	Victim is 12 and un- der 16: 20Y. Vic- tim is 16 and under 18: 10Y. If defend- and is 17 and under 21, penalty is $500	§435.080 — Rape of victim under 12: death or life; attempt: 20Y §435.100 — Intercourse with vic- tim under 12: death or 20 to 50Y
Louisiana	c14§80	Victim 12 but under 17, defendant over 17: 5Y	c14§42 — Victim under 12: death only
Maine	c130§11	Victim is between 14 and 16: $500 or 2Y	c130§10 — Victim under 14: any term of years c130§12 — Assault with intent to commit, victim un- der 14: 20Y

	Citation	Penalty	Citation & Penalty	
Maryland	Art. 27 §464	Victim is between 14 and 16: $500 a/o 2Y	Art. 27 §462	Victim under 14: court may sentence defendant to death, life, or not more than 21Y; but if jury specifies "without capital punishment," maximum is 20Y
			Art. 27§12	Assault with intent to commit, victim is under 14: 10Y
Mass.	c272§4	Victim is under 18: $1000 a/o 3Y	c265§23	Victim under 16: life
			c265§24B	Assault with intent to commit, victim under 16: life
Mich.	§28.341	Accosting, enticing or soliciting child under 16 for sexual intercourse: 1: 1Y; 2: felony		
	§28.571	Female defendant over 15 and male victim under 15: 5Y		
	§28.574	Guardian and ward: $5000 or 10Y		
	§28.788	Victim is under 16: Life or any term of years or indeterminate sentence 1D to life if found to be "sexually delinquent person" [§28.200 (1)]		
Minnesota	§617.02	Victim under 10: life	§617.02	Col. 2
		Victim under 14: 30Y Victim under 18: 7Y		
Mississippi	§559.260	Victim over 12 but under 18: $500 a/o 6M or 5Y in pen	§2358	Victim under 12: death, or if jury decide, life
	§1999	Teacher & pupil; teacher: $500 A 6M; pupil: $500		
Missouri	§559.260	Victim under 16: death or not less than 2Y in discretion of jury		
	§559.320	Guardian & ward: 5Y in pen or 1Y in county jail and not less than $100 plus loss of civil rights, §559.470	§559.470	

	Citation	Penalty	Citation & Penalty
Montana	§94-4101 (1)	99Y	
Nebraska	§28-408	20Y	
Nevada	§200.360	Penalty as provided for forcible rape (5Y-life) or violent rape (20Y-death)	§207.020 Victim under 10: court may order sterilization in addition to other penalty
New Hamp-shire	§585:16 §173:3	Victim under 16: 30Y Sexual psychopath act inquiry discretionary	§173:3 Where defendant charged with "enticing child" sexual psychopath act inquiry is mandatory
N. J.	§2A:138-1	Defendant 16 or over and victim is under 12: $5000 a/o 30Y; same but victim is under 16: $5000 a/o 15Y	§2A:138-1 Victim under 12: $5-000 a/o 30Y
	§2A:90-2	Assault with intent to commit rape: $3000 a/o 12Y	
N.M.	§40-39-1	Victim under 16: 1 to 99Y	§40-39-2 Victim under 10: life
	§40-39-8	Teacher and pupil: 5Y	
N.Y.	Penal §201	Defendant 21 or over and victim is under 18, offense is rape II and penalty is 10Y; where circumstances do not amount to rape II (i.e., defendant is under 21?), offense is misdemeanor rape and penalty is $500 a/o 1Y	
	Penal §243	Assault II with intent to commit rape II: life indeterminate	
	Penal §1940	Second offense of rape II: life indeterminate; second offense of violation of §243: life indeterminate	
	CCP§552	Misdemeanor rape not bailable where defendant has two prior convictions of certain listed misdemeanors or of any felony	
North Caro-lina	§14-26	Victim over 12 and under 16: felony* Female defendant and male victim under 16: misdem*	§14-21 Victim under 12: death, or if jury recommend, life

109

	Citation	Penalty	Citation & Penalty
continued	§14-27	Male defendant less than 18 and victim over 12 and under 16: misdemeanor°	

°Felony and misdemeanor punishable in discretion of court

	Citation	Penalty	Citation & Penalty
North Dakota		Victim is under 18, and:	
	§§12-30-04,-05	Where defendant is 24 or over, first degree rape: not less than 1Y	
	§§12-30-06,-07	Where defendant is 20 and less than 24, second degree rape: not less than 1Y	
	§§12-30-60-,80	Defendant is less than 20, third degree rape: 3Y in training school	
	§12-30-10	Guardian and ward; or with inmate of institution, or when administering welfare: 15Y	
	§12-30-12	Board of pardons may order psychiatric treatment	
Ohio	§2905.03	Victim under 16: 20Y in pen or 6M in county jail	§2905.02 Forcible, and victim is under 12, life is mandatory
	§2905.04	Attempt at, defendant is 18 or over and victim is under 16: 15Y in pen or 6M in county jail	
	§2905.13	Tutor and pupil: 10Y	
Oklahoma	T21§§1111, 1112, 1114, 1116	Where defendant is under 18 and victim is under 16; or where victim is over 16 but under 18 and chaste, offense is second degree rape: 15Y	T21§§ 1111, 1115 Where defendant is over 18 and victim under 14, offense is first degree: death or not less than 15Y
			T21§1123 Proposal of, to victim under 14: 20Y
Oregon	§163.210	Defendant over 16; victim under 18: 20Y	
	§167.030	Defendant over 18; victim is 16 but under 18: 5Y pen or $500 or 1Y in county jail	

110

	Citation	Penalty	EXTRAORDINARY PENALTY WHERE VICTIM IS UNDER CERTAIN AGE (Forcible intercourse not distinguished) Citation & Penalty
Pennsylvania	T18 §4721	Victim under 16: $7-000 a/o 15Y solitary and hard labor	
Puerto Rico	T33 §§961 (1), 964	Victim under 14: not less than 1Y	
Rhode Island	§11-37-2 §11-37-3 §11-37-4	Victim under 16: 15Y Attempt: 10Y Defendant over 18; victim under 18: 5Y	
South Carolina	Constitution Art. 3 §33 §16-80	14 is age of consent Victim under 16: Death unless jury designate mercy, in which case 40Y at hard labor; victim over 10: if jury recommend mercy, 14Y; victim over 14 but under 16: 5Y; if defendant is under 18 and victim over 14 and unchaste: $500 or 1Y	
South Dakota	§§13.2801 to 2803	Victim under 18: 20Y	§§13.2801 to 2803 Victim under 10: not less than 10Y
Tennessee	§39-3706	Victim over 12 and under 21: 10Y; where victim under 14, reputation for unchastity not admissible	§39-3705 Victim under 12: death, but jury may commute to not less than 10Y
	§39-3707	Parent consenting or aiding violation of §3706 is deemed a principal	§39-606 AWITC, victim under 12: 21Y
Texas	PC Art. 1183, 1189	Victim under 18: death or not less than 5Y	PC Art. 1183 Victim under 15: defendant cannot show lack of chastity as defense
Utah	§76-53-19 §§77-49-1	Victim over 13 and under 18: 5Y Presentence mental examination	§§76-53-15, -18 Victim under 13: 20Y to life
Vermont	T13 §3201	Defendant over 16, victim under 16: misdemeanor* and defendant may be committed to "Weeks" school	

*Semble no statutory penalty

	Citation	Penalty	WHERE VICTIM IS UNDER CERTAIN AGE EXTRAORDINARY PENALTY (Forcible intercourse not distinguished) Citation & Penalty
Virginia	§18.1-44	Consenting victim 14 but under 16: 20Y	§18.1-44 Semble, where victim under 14: death or not less than 5Y
	§18.1-46	If victim 14 but under 16 is found of bad moral repute or lewd, defendant is not guilty of rape, but jury may convict defendant of contributing to delinquency or of fornication	
	See §18.1-14	Attempting to h a v e sexual intercourse with female under 18 not of previous chaste character or who was previously married: $500 a/o 12M	
Wash.	§9.79.020	Victim 10 and under 15: 20Y Victim 15 and under 18: 15Y	§9.79.020 Victim under 10: life
W. Va.	§5930	Male defendant over 16; female victim u n d e r 16 and chaste: death or life in court's discretion, or if jury recommend mercy, 5 to 20Y; Same, but sexes reversed: 6M; where male defendant under 16 and victim over 12 who consents, semble, no crime	
Wisconsin	§944.10	Victim u n d e r 18: $1000 a/o 5Y; defendant 18 and up, victim under 16: 15Y; defendant 18 and up, victim under 12: 30Y	
	§959.15	Discretionary presentence mental examination a n d treatment	
Wyoming	§6-63 §6-97	Victim under 18: life Carnal knowledge of female prisoner: 5Y	
	§§7-348 to 362	Presentence m e n t a l examination a n d treatment in lieu of penalty if found to be within sex offender act.	

112

Table 5
INCEST

	Citation	Penalty
Alabama	T14 §325	7Y
Alaska	§65-4-13	Incestuous rape of daughter or sister; defendant over 19: any term of years; defendant under 19: 20Y
	§65-9-9	15Y
Arizona	§13-471	10Y
Arkansas	§§41-811, 812 §§55-103, 105	10Y Incestuous marriage: fine a/o imprisonment in discretion of jury
California	Penal §285 Penal §11112	50Y Fingerprinting
Colorado	§40-9-4 §40-9-5 §40-9-6 §39-10-18	Marriage is void Incestuous marriage: $500 or 5Y Father on daughter: father gets 20Y Loss of civil rights
Connecticut	§35-223	10Y
Delaware	T11 §591	$500 and 7Y
District of Columbia	§22-1901	12Y
Florida	§741.21 §741.22	Marriage prohibited 20Y
Georgia	§26-5701 §26-5702	20Y Incestuous marriage: 3Y
Hawaii	§309-21	$500 or 10Y
Idaho	§18-6602	10Y
Illinois	c38 §374 c38 §375 c38 §587	Father on daughter: 20Y All other: 10Y Person convicted is infamous and suffers certain disabilities, as to which see Table 1
	c38 §785 c108 §106	No probation Confinement in special division of prison
Indiana	§10-4206	21Y
Iowa	§704.1	25Y
Kansas	§21-906	7Y
Kentucky	§436.060	21Y
Louisiana	c14 §78	15Y
Maine	c134 §2	10Y
Maryland	Art. 27 §335	10Y
Mass.	c272 §17	20Y

113

	Citation	Penalty
Mich.	§28.565	10Y; or indeterminate sentence 1D to life if found to be "sexually delinquent person" [§28.200 (1)]
Minnesota	§617.13	10Y
Miss.	§2000	Incestuous lewd cohabitation: 10Y
	§2234	$500 a/o 10Y
Missouri	§563.220	7Y
Montana	§94-705	10Y
Nebraska	§28-407	Father on daughter or brother on sister (incestuous rape): life [To be distinguished from incest: Toth v. State, 141 Neb. 448, 3 N.W. 2d 899.]
	§28-905	15Y
	§28-906	Father on daughter, "licentiously cohabiting": 20Y
	§83-504	Castration
Nevada	§201.180	10Y
New Hampshrie	§579.7	$1000 a/o 20Y
	§173:3	Sexual psychopath act inquiry discretionary
New Jersey	§2A:114-1	$1000 a/o 5Y
	§2A:114-2	With own child: $1000 a/o 15Y
New Mexico	§40-6-3	50Y
New York	Penal §1110	10Y
North Carolina	§14-178	15Y
	§14-179	Uncle on niece; aunt on nephew: misdemeanor punished in discretion of court
North Dakota	§12-22-06	10Y
Ohio	§2905.02	Incestuous rape of daughter or sister: life mandatory
	§2905.07	10Y
	§2951.04	No probation
Oklahoma	T21 §885	10Y
Oregon	§137.111	Victim under 16, court may give indeterminate life sentence
	§137.112	Victim under 16, psychiatric examination is necessary
	§167.035	3Y pen or 1Y county jail or $1000; detention, enticement or victim under 16 by defendant over 16 with intent to commit, 5Y or indeterminate life
	§163.220	Incestuous rape: life
	§167.050	Second offense, or prior conviction of certain other crimes: life indeterminate

114

	Citation	**Penalty**
Penn.	T18 §4507	$2000 a/o 5Y solitary at hard labor
	T19 §1081	No probation
	T19 §§1166 to 74	Indeterminate life sentence in court's discretion; psychiatric examination
	T18 §5110	Where defendant over 21 has accomplice under 18, penalty may be doubled
Puerto Rico	T33 §1115	(Includes marriage) 10Y
Rhode Island	§11-6-4	10Y
	§15-1-4	Jews permitted to marry within degrees of consanguinity
South Carolina	§16-402	Not less than $500 a/o not less than 1Y
	Constitution Art. 2, §6	Conviction for, disqualifies one as elector
South Dakota	§13.1715	10Y, but if victim is under 10 or incapable of consenting thru lunacy: not less than 10Y
Tennessee	§39-705	21Y
	§39-706	Begetting child on wife's sister: 10Y
Texas	PC Art 495	10Y
	CCP Art 776	No suspended sentence
Utah	§76-53-4	15Y
	§§77-49-1 to 8	Presentence mental examination
Vermont	T13 §205	"same as adultery" Note: there are two penalties for adultry: §202 is $1000 a/o 5Y; §203 is $1000
Virginia	§18.1-191	Father on daughter or granddaughter / Mother on son or grandson / Daughter on father / Son on mother } 10Y in pen or $1000 a/o 12M
		All others: $500 a/o 12M
Washington	§9.79.090	Victim under 10: semble life mandatory
		Victim 10 and under 15: 20Y
		Vicitm 15 and under 18: 15Y
		If both parties 18 & up, both get 15Y
	§§71.06.010 to 140	Post conviction or acquittal examination for sexual psychopathy
West Virginia	§6067	10Y
	§§2666 (1) ff	Mandatory sex offender examination
Wisconsin	§944.06	10Y
	§959.15	Discretionary presentence mental examination
Wyoming	§6-85	5Y in pen or 12M in county jail
	§§7-348 to 362	Presentence mental examination and treatment in lieu of penalty if found to be within sex offender act

Table 6

	A ADULTERY Citation	A ADULTERY Penalty	B FORNICATION Citation	B FORNICATION Penalty	C LEWD COHABITATION Citation	C LEWD COHABITATION Penalty
Alabama	T14 §16	1: not less than $100 and discretionary 6M; 2: with same person, not less than $300 & discretionary 12M; 3: 2Y	T14 §16	Col. 2		
Alaska	§65-9-1 §65-9-2	Negro and white: 7Y $200 or 3M Adultery includes offense of unmarried man with married woman	T14 §360	Col. 2	§65-9-3	2Y
Arizona	§13-221	3Y			§13-222	3Y
Arkansas			Same applies to fornication, see Ex Parte Isojoki, 222 F. 151 (1922)		§41-805 §41-806 §41-810	1: $100; 2: not less than $100 and discretionary 12M; 3: 3Y Negro and white: 1Y Delivery of mulatto child is prima facie evidence
California		Indictable only as lewd cohabitation, People v. Woodson, 156 P. 278 (1916)			PC §269a PC §269b	$1000 a/o 1Y $500 a/o 6M
Colorado					§40-9-3	$200 or 6M (multiply penalty for repeat violations)
Connecticut	§53-218	5Y	§53-219	$100 a/o 6M	§53-222	Abandon spouse and cohabit with another: 3Y

State	Citation	Penalty	Citation	Penalty	Citation	Penalty / Notes
Delaware	T11 §311	$500 a/o 1Y				
District of Columbia	§22-301	$500 a/o 1Y	§22-1002			$500 a/o 1Y
Florida	§798.03	$300 a/o 6M		$30 or 3M	§798.01 $500 or 2Y; §798.02 $300 or 2Y; §798.04 White and negro: $1000 or 12M; §798.05 Same: $500 or 12M	
Georgia	§26-58	$1000 a/o 12M	§26-5801			
Hawaii	§§309-8, 309-9	Male: $100 a/o 12M; Female: $30 or 4M	§§309-10, 309-12	$50 or 3M	§309-15 Aiding, of female under 18: 3Y	§309-11 Cohabitation after divorce carries same penalty as adultery
Idaho	§18-6601	$1000 or 3Y	§18-6603	$300 a/o 6M	§18-6604 $300 a/o 6M; §§34-404 Not permitted to vote; penalty for violation: $500 a/o 6M	
Illinois	c4 §9.1 — Fornication and adultery punishable only when openly practiced: Chicago v. Murray, 333 Ill. App. 233, 77 NE 2d 452		c4 §9.1	"Unfit" for adoption purposes	c38 §46	1: $500 or 1Y; 2: multiply penalty (Col. 2)
Indiana	§10-4207 — Indictable only where there is cohabitation, State v. Chandler, 96 Ind. 591; but cohabitation need not be open, Richey v. State, 172 Ind. 134	$500 a/o 6M				
Iowa	§702.1, §21-908	3Y				
Kansas	§21-908	$500 a/o 6M	§21-908	Col. 2	§21-908	Col. 2

	A ADULTERY		B FORNICATION		C LEWD COHABITATION	
	Citation	Penalty	Citation	Penalty	Citation	Penalty
Kentucky	§436.070	$50	§436.070	Col. 2	§402.990	Cohabitation after conviction for miscegenous marriage: 12M
Louisiana	Civil Code Art 161	Where divorced guilty party marries accomplice, bigamy: 5Y (c14 §76)				
Maine	c134 §1	$1000 or 5Y	c134 §8		c134 §5	$300 or 5Y
Maryland	Art 27 §4	$10	Art 27 §416	$100 and 60D Woman permitting self to be got pregnant by negro: 5Y (held unconstitutional)		
Massachusetts	c272 §14 c273 §11	$500 or 3Y Getting a woman pregnant: misdemeanor (semble no statutory penalty)	c272 §18 c273 §11	$30 or 3M Col. 2	c272 §16	$300 or 2Y
Michigan	§28.219	$2000 a/o 4Y			§28.567 §28.221	$500 or 1Y Cohabitation by divorced persons: $2000 a/o 4Y
Minnesota	§617.15	$300 or 2Y	§617.16 §7156	$100 or 90D Hotel may eject couple	§1998 §2000	$500 and 6M Incestuous or miscegenous: 10Y $1000 a/o 1Y
Mississippi					§563.150	
Missouri			Not an offense, St. v. Chandler, 132 Mo. 155, 33 SW 797 §6-86			
Montana					§94-4107	$500 a/o 6M
Nebraska	§28-902	1Y			§28-928	$100 and 6M
Nevada					§201.200	$1000 a/o 1Y
N. Hampshire	§579:1	$500 and 1Y; or 3Y §579:4		$50 or 6M		

118

State	Statute	Penalty	Statute	Penalty / Notes	Further provisions
New Jersey	§2A:88-1	$1000 a/o 3Y	§2A:110-1		§2A:115-1 $1000 a/o 3Y; §2A:133-4 With compulsion $2000 a/o 7Y
New Mexico	§40-7-2			$50 a/o 6M	$80; but couple can avoid penalty by marriage or separation if there be impediment
New York	Penal §102	$250 a/o 6M			°Misdemeanor punished in discretion of court
N. Carolina	§§14-186 and 72-37	Falsely registering in hotel as husband and wife: misdem°	§14-184	Misdem°	
N. Dakota	§§12-22-09, 10, 11	$500 a/o 3Y pen or 1Y county jail	§12-22-08	Where defendant is over 18: $100; defendant under 18 is proceeded against under laws relating to juvenile courts	§12-22-12 $500 or 1Y; §12-22-13 Negro and white not lawfully married, occupying same room: $500 a/o 1Y
Ohio	§2905.08	$200 and 3M	§2905.08	Col. 2	§2905.17 Compel cohabitation: $1000 and 10Y
Oklahoma	T21 §§871, 872	$500 a/o 5Y	see T21 §871	$500 a/o 5Y	§871
Oregon	§167.005	2Y in pen or 1Y in county jail or $1000	§167.030	Defendant is over 18; victim is 16 but under 18: $500 or 1Y in county jail or 5Y in pen	§167.015 $300 or 6M
Pennsylvania	T18 §4505	$500 a/o 1Y	T18 §4506	$100	
Puerto Rico	T33 §1081	$2000 or 5Y	§11-6-3	$10	
R. Island	§11-6-2	$500 or 1Y	§16-408°		Must be habitual: §§16-407, 408°
S. Carolina	§16-406°	Must be habitual: $500 a/o 1Y	§16-408°	Must be habitual: $500 a/o 1Y	Adultery (§407) and fornication (§408) where parties live together: $500 a/o 1Y

°Conviction disqualifies one as elector, Constitution Art. 2 §6

	A		B		C	
	ADULTERY		**FORNICATION**		**LEWD COHABITATION**	
	Citation	Penalty	Citation	Penalty	Citation	Penalty
S. Dakota	§§13.3001, .3002	$500 a/o 5Y				
Tennessee						
Texas	PC Arts. 499, 502	Must be habitual: $1000	PC Arts. 503, 504	Must be habitual $500	PC Arts. 499, 502 PC Arts. 503, 504	One or both is married to another (adultery): $1000. Both unmarried: $500
Utah	§76-53-3	3Y	§76-53-5	$100 or 6M	see §76-39-1(1)	$300 a/o 6M
Vermont	T13 §201 T13 §203	$1000 a/o 5Y Found in bed together: $1000			T13 §204	Parties to divorce or annulled marriage who cohabit: $500
Virginia	§18.1-41 §18.1-190 §18.1-192	Married male and single female: 10Y $100 Conspiracy to cause spouse to commit: 10Y; other party gets 5Y	§18.1-190	$100	§18.1-193	Includes married guilty of lasciviousness: 1: $500; 2: $500 and discretionary 12M
Washington	§9.79.110	$1000 or 2Y			§9.79.120	$1000 a/o 1Y
W. Virginia	§5169 §6058	(Justice court): $20 $1000 a/o 3Y	§5169 §6058	(Justice court): $20 $200 a/o 6M	§6059	1: $50 and discretionary 6M; 2: 12M
Wisconsin	§944.16	Discretionary presentence examination + treatment	§944.15	Col. 2	§944.20(3)	$500 a/o 1Y
	§959.15		§959.15		§247.39	Cohabitation after divorce $1000 a/o 3Y
					§959.15	Col. 2
Wyoming	§6-86	Only where cohabitation; $100 and 3M	§6-86	Only where cohabitation; $100 and 3M	§6-86	Cohabitation in state of adultery or fornication: $100 and 3M

INDEX

LEGAL ALMANAC SERIES CONVERSION TABLE
List of Present Titles and Authors

LEGAL ALMANAC SERIES CONVERSION TABLE
List of Original Titles and Authors